CASTILE

PHILIP'S TRAVEL GUIDES

CASTILE

James Bentley

Photography by Joe Cornish

GEORGE
PHILIP

Acknowledgements

I must express my gratitude to Jennifer Paton, marketing director of The Magic of Spain, 227 Shepherd's Bush Road, London W6 7AS. I also remain extremely grateful for the help I have received from Chantal Weatherley-White, PR director of the Spanish National Tourist Office in London, and from the director of the Tourist Office, Sr German Porras.

British Library Cataloguing in Publication Data
Bentley, James *1937–*

Castile. – (Philip's travel guides)
1. Castile (Spain). Travel
I. Title
946.30483

ISBN 0–540–01249–1

Text © James Bentley 1991
Photographs © Joe Cornish 1991
Maps © George Philip 1991

First published by George Philip Limited,
59 Grosvenor Street, London W1X 9DA

Typeset by Keyspools Ltd, Golborne, Lancs
Printed in Italy

Contents

Author's dedication

For Andrew Best
for many years my patient literary agent

Photographer's dedication

The photographs in this book are dedicated to Jenny with
my heartfelt thanks; she was with me at the making of
almost every one of them, her vision quietly contributing,
and her loyal companionship making life 'on the road'
worth living.

Half-title illustration **Storks survey the morning from the Cordoban-style tower of the church of San Miguel at Almazán.**

Title-page illustration **A remote fortress stands sentinel above the Oza valley south of Ponferrada.**

Opposite **The wide thoroughfare at Castrillo de los Polvazares, one of the finest surviving *Maragatos* villages, curves past the church of Santa Catalina.**

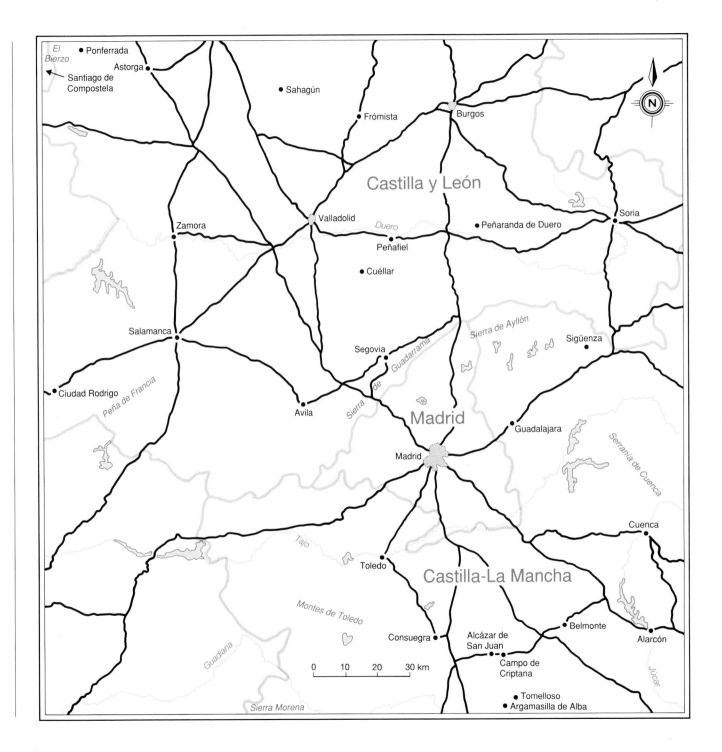

El
Bierzo

• Ponferrada

Astorga •

Santiago de
Compostela

• Sahagún

Frómista •

Burgos

Castilla y León

Zamora •

Valladolid

Duero

• Peñaranda de Duero

Soria

Peñafiel •

• Cuéllar

Sierra de Ayllón

Salamanca •

Sigüenza •

Segovia •

Sierra de Guadarrama

• Ciudad Rodrigo

Peña de Francia

Madrid

Avila •

Sierra

Madrid

Guadalajara •

Serranía de Cuenca

Cuenca •

Tajo

Toledo •

Castilla-La Mancha

Montes de Toledo

Belmonte •

Guadiana

Consuegra •

Alcázar de
San Juan

Alarcón •

| 0 | 10 | 20 | 30 km |

Campo de
Criptana

Júcar

Sierra Morena

• Tomelloso
• Argamasilla de Alba

Introduction

Castile is huge, made up of two of the seventeen autonomous regions of Spain. With its five provinces, the smaller of the two, Castilla-La Mancha, covers more than 79 square kilometres. Castilla y León, the largest of all the autonomies of Spain, extends over more than 94 square kilometres and embraces nine provinces.

Geographically the land is diverse. Castilla-La Mancha derives part of its name from the Arabic word *manxu*, 'arid', and huge stretches of it are parched and dusty. Yet the longest river in the peninsula, the Tajo (or Tagus), bisects Castilla-La Mancha by way of a series of deep gorges, secluded woodland valleys and the occasional huge artificial lake. Between the Tajo and the Río Guadiana are the Montes de Toledo, which constitute the oldest range in the whole Iberian peninsula. Designated a wildlife reserve, they are a magnet for ornithologists. The Sierra Morena closes off the southern part of the region from the rest of Spain.

Castilla y León is similarly crossed from east to west by a superb river, the Duero, which has so many tributaries that the Castilians have put into its mouth the claim, 'I am the Duero which drinks all waters'. Castilla y León includes the backbone of Spain, a central mass of mountainous land extending from the Sierra de Ayllón in the east and running westwards to incorporate the Sierra de Guadarrama, the Sierra de Gredos, the Sierra de Béjar and, on the Portuguese border, the Peña de Francia. For those who venture into the remoter regions, the sight of wildlife is complemented by the often spectacular Castilian panoramas.

Roe deer, red partridge, lynx, wild turkey, fallow deer, wild boar, stags, foxes and pigeons populate the mountainous forests, while buzzards and eagles float lazily in the sky. The more adventurous visitors canoe down the Guadiana and the upper reaches of the Tajo, along routes which in the past were taken by loggers who would lash pines together and float rafts down as far as Aranjuez.

In many parts of this territory the wildlife has the land to itself. Castilla y León, for example, has a population of no more than 2.6 million people, giving a density per square kilometre of approximately one third of the national average. In consequence, in addition to its wealth of world-renowned and astonishingly beautiful cities, such as Toledo, Salamanca, Burgos, Avila and Segovia, much of Castile is completely unspoilt and virtually undiscovered. Both regions comprise high moorlands, flat plains, fertile pasturelands, and fields of vines, olives and cereals. At times one wonders how the farmers manage to coax their seed to germinate in the rocky terrain of mountain pastures. Sometimes the landscape is bleak and entirely inhospitable. Elsewhere pine forests give way to beech trees and cork oaks, to elms and chestnuts, to ilexes and junipers.

In certain areas, such as El Bierzo, west of León, the micro-climate is oceanic, the temperature mild, the rainfall refreshing. But for the most part Castile is high above sea level. Sixty-five per cent of Castilla y León consists of upland plateaux, the limestone plains in the east and north rising from 850 to 1000 metres, the mountain plains to the west scarcely ever lower. What are called the foothills are even higher, starting at 900 metres and rising to 1100; and even the farmlands start at 700 metres.

As a result Castile is a land of exceedingly cold winters and hot summers. The French poet and novelist Théophile Gautier, who visited Spain one summer in the mid nineteenth century, observed that the pavements of many a *plazuela* or street open to the glare of the sun were so hot that showmen could make geese and turkeys dance on them, and wretched dogs rushed across them howling plaintively. 'If you lift a doorknocker, you burn your fingers, and you can feel your brains boiling in your skull like a stewpot on a fire', he noted. 'Your nose turns cardinal red, and your body evaporates in sweat.'

Yet he was also aware that the narrow streets of Toledo, where people in houses facing each other could join hands across the road, were entirely suited to such a torrid climate. 'At the bottom of these narrow clefts, slicing at exactly the right angles through the blocks and islands of houses, you enjoy a deliciously cool shade.' In addition, of course, the Castilians take a siesta during the most uncomfortable period of the day, and they eat late, when the intense heat has been dissipated. Another device for escaping the worst rigours of the climate is that exquisite piece of urban architecture, the flower-filled patio, or courtyard. This really provides the Spaniards with two houses in one, enabling them to live on the cool ground floor during the summer and to transfer to the warm upper storey during the colder months.

Whatever the climate, as numerous prehistoric cave

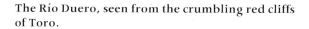

The Río Duero, seen from the crumbling red cliffs of Toro.

The remains of Roman houses line the roads of Numancia.

paintings have demonstrated, men and women have lived here for millennia. At Saelices, in the province of Guadalajara, is the first known depiction of love-making in the history of art, and in a cave in the mountains near Nerpio, in the province of Albacete, is a prehistoric carving of a mountain goat.

Inevitably the Romans left an indelible imprint on Castile. At Numancia, 7 kilometres north of Soria, for example, excavation has revealed one of the most evocative Roman sites in the region. In 134 BC the Celtic-Iberian fortified town of Numancia was the scene of a heroic struggle, when its inhabitants took on the army of Scipio Aemilianus, victor of Carthage; after nearly a year's hopeless resistance, rather than surrender they committed suicide by flinging themselves into a furnace. The Romans then proceeded to lay out their own grid-shaped camp on the site of the previous settlement. Archaeologists have uncovered beneath the Celtic-Iberian town the remains of even earlier

Ancient stone shepherds' huts at Antilla del Pina,
10 kilometres west of Palencia.

prehistoric houses. Many Roman legacies survived intact longer than Numancia. The walls of Astorga and of Avila still rise from Roman foundations, and the aqueduct of Segovia is one of the most astonishing legacies of the Trajan era in the Roman world. At Medinaceli the second-century AD triumphal arch is the only one with three arches still standing in Spain.

Roman roads crisscross the region, as do ancient shepherd tracks. Semi-nomadic shepherds no longer drive huge flocks of merinos twice a year from northern to southern Spain as they used to, and today these tracks, known as *cañadas* because they were once fenced with canes, are difficult to spot with an inexperienced eye. Yet as the traveller drives along the relatively modern and ever improving roads of Castile, flocks of sheep, sometimes guarded by a single man and a dog, can still be seen, often perilously close to the roadside, following their traditional paths. Though the canes have now disappeared, what still remain dotted about the countryside are many ancient, conical shepherds' huts.

Later, pilgrimage routes developed, above all those to Santiago de Compostela. This pilgrimage added new legends to Spanish history and provided sculptors and painters with a new iconography. Traditionally, Jesus's apostle St James the Great is said to have spent seven years preaching the gospel in Galicia before returning to Jerusalem, where he was executed in AD 44 by King Herod Agrippa I. Then in the ninth century the appearance of a star led Bishop Theodomir of Irinese to a wild spot near the Spanish coast where a hermit claimed to have discovered the body of the saint. Over this grave King Alfonso III of Asturias built a sanctuary, and the town that grew around it became known as St James of the Field of the Star, or Santiago de Compostela.

Soon, along with Rome and Jerusalem, the shrine had become one of the three major centres of Christian pilgrimage. Then, during the reign of Ramiro I, St James the Great made a yet more miraculous appearance. In 844, as the forces of Ramiro were engaging the Moorish troops of Abd ar-Rahman II at the battle of Clavijo, the apostle appeared at the king's side, riding a white charger and slaying countless Moors. Santiago thus became the patron saint of Spain. Endlessly depicted in cathedrals and churches, carved over the doorways of hospices and portrayed by Spain's greatest artists, he appears in several guises: as an apostle and writer, sitting with the New Testament epistle attributed to him; as a pilgrim, staff and scrip in hand, and with a cockle shell, the symbol of St James and his pilgrims to Compostela, on his pilgrim's hat; and as the *Matamoros*, the Moor-slayer, his prancing charger battering the corpses of decapitated Moors.

Castile is a land of countless isolated hermitages, where holy men and women sought refuge from the cares of the world to devote themselves to God. With the cult of Santiago de Compostela, new religious

Shaded by trees, the little romanesque chapel of San Miguel stands just outside Población de Campos.

At Quintanilla de las Viñas the style of these seventh-century Visigothic carvings in the hermitage chapel testifies to byzantine influences on early Spanish Christianity.

foundations began to appear alongside them. Hospices were built to shelter pilgrims; commanderies of knights were formed, dedicated to protecting them on their journey; and bridges, sometimes fortified, were erected, often as pious gifts by monarchs to ease the pilgrims' passage across the rivers along their way. To benefit from the indulgences available for those who completed all or part of the pilgrimage, official certificates along the route were granted to those who passed by. Some spots, such as the chapel of San Miguel outside Población de Campos, became notorious for granting fake certificates.

Another group of travellers has also bequeathed its modest legacy to Castile. In the Middle Ages an ancient tribe which had inhabited this region since pre-Roman times, desperate for food, abandoned traditional farming and became muleteers. These *Maragatos* have given the name La Maragatería to the region of Castilla y León that lies between León and El Bierzo. Such villages as Castrillos de Los Polvazares, just west of Astorga, have main streets built wide enough to accommodate the passing of mule trains.

The most turbulent periods of Spanish history have of course left a permanent mark on the region. The Romans did not manage to preserve peace by themselves, and were obliged to call the Visigoths from southern Gaul to put down the Franks and the Vandals who were ravaging the land. The Franks, who proved difficult to conquer, managed to force the Visigoths to take refuge in Spain. Riven by religious controversies, this militaristic race accepted orthodox Catholicism only after the third Council of Toledo in 589.

They too have left us some fascinating remains (a not too overwhelming collection is on display in the romanesque church of San Román in Toledo), and sometimes they have been discovered in the most unexpected places. In 1156 Alfonso VII gave his blessing to the building of a convent on the left bank of the Río Duero, south of Peñaranda de Duero. Successive rebuilding resulted in the now majestic church of Santa María de La Vid (St Mary of the Vine). Only in the late 1980s was it discovered that the convent of 1156 must have risen on an earlier one, for restoration work in the cloister has revealed Visigothic arches, columns and capitals.

Another Visigothic survival in Castile almost perished in the waters of a twentieth-century reservoir. Happily the late seventh-century sanctuary of San Pedro de la Nave in the Esla valley was dismantled and re-erected at El Campillo, a dozen kilometres north-west of Zamora. A yet more fascinating Visigothic survival, for a number of reasons, is San Juan Bautista de Baños, 10 kilometres south of Palencia. In the first place, despite its dedication to St John the Baptist, this sanctuary was founded in 661 by a Visigothic king in thanksgiving after his sight had

Visigothic arches, columns and capitals in the cloister of the eleventh-century monastery at La Vid.

been restored by a goddess who watched over a medicinal spring. Secondly, the church symbolically celebrates the triumph of the Visigoths by cannibalizing materials from a previous building which stood on this spot. Thirdly, it represents their decline by incorporating one of the horseshoe arches so much favoured by their conquerors, the Moors.

This mixture of Arabs (initially chiefly Yemeni) and Berbers from north Africa began conquering Spain in 711 and was not finally driven out until 1492. The invaders left an indelible mark on the region. At first they prayed in what had been Visigothic churches, but only until they had either transformed them into mosques or built new ones. The Visigothic horseshoe arch, immensely refined, became one of their favourite motifs, and they introduced multi-lobed and super-imposed arches, which were sometimes supported by forests of columns. Byzantine artists were brought to Spain to embellish their mosques and castles with marble and gold.

The name Castile was still to come. Around 800 it was first applied to a district to the north of Burgos, at the foot of the Cantabrian mountains. As the region expanded, it was plagued by the squabbles of rulers nominally under the suzerainty of the kings of Asturias and León. Fernán González, who died in 970, was the first count of all Castile. Establishing his capital at Burgos, he and his immediate successors made some headway in reconquering Castile from the Moors. Sancho the Great of Navarre managed to split Castile from León, and his second son declared himself King Ferdinando I of Castile. But continual strife between the rival sovereigns long delayed the reconquest.

As its new name implied, Castile was already a land of castles. The Moors built many more, and *alcázar*, the word for fortress in Spanish, is Arabic in origin. Usually Moorish fortresses differed from those built by the Christians in lacking a keep, instead relying for their defence on towers, which were all of the same height, and an enormous bailey. An *albacar*, surrounded by a defensive wall, enabled those who lived in villages outside the fortress to take refuge when

threatened with attack. In Castilla-La Mancha the most solid Moorish base was Toledo, which they held for three centuries. Here they built a mosque which the Christians later transformed into the church of Santo Cristo de la Luz without destroying the cupolas which mimic the style favoured by the caliphs of Córdoba.

The Moors also founded Magerit (later Madrid), and in the 850s Emir Mohammed I ringed the city with walls and gave it a fortress, which stood till it was consumed by fire on Christmas night, 1724. At Segovia in Castilla y León, Abd ar-Rahman III, Caliph of Córdoba, built an *alcázar* which formed the basis of successive rebuildings, by Alfonso VI at the end of the eleventh century, Enrique II of Castile in the mid fourteenth century and Catherine of Lancaster (the wife of Enrique III) in the fifteenth.

Up to 500 castles and fortresses remain standing in Castilla-La Mancha alone. Of the 450 or so surviving in Castilla y León, some 200 are either still in excellent condition or have been restored. The massive fortress of Guadamur, south-west of Toledo, seems not to have changed since Pedro López de Ayala built it in the mid fifteenth century. Six turrets still protect its huge crenellated keep, and even larger towers, round and triangular, defend its dressed stone walls. In fact French troops set it on fire during the Napoleonic Wars, and it was again sacked during the Carlist civil wars; what we see today is a faithful nineteenth-century reconstruction. As for the celebrated *alcázar* of Toledo, it had to be almost entirely rebuilt after Colonel Moscardó made it his base in the uprising of 1936 against the republican government.

Pedro López de Ayala built his fortress on the remains of a Moorish stronghold, and many Castilian fortresses still retain Moorish names: the fortress of Alarcón, for example, which glowers from its rocky eminence over pine trees and a lake formed by the turbulent Río Júcar as it tumbles down from the hills of the Serranía de Cuenca. Long an Arab stronghold,

Extremely playful gothic designs surround the windows of the castle at Belmonte.

it was taken by the Christians in 1184, when the legendary Fernán Martínez de Ceballos scaled its walls at night by striking his daggers into the mortar between the rugged stones of the fortress, climbed the battlements and opened the gates for his fellow Castilians. Alarcón, in spite of its still formidable appearance, is now a National Parador, one of a series of state-run hotels throughout the country, many of them converted from historic buildings – castles, palaces and convents – in spectacular situations.

When the celebrated film starring Charlton Heston as El Cid and Sophia Loren as his wife was shot in Spain in the 1960s the producers chose the magical castle of Belmonte, near Cuenca, as the scene of his exploits. El Cid in fact met his death at Valencia on 10 July 1099 and this particular fortress, with its barbicans, towers and battlements, was not built until the fifteenth century. In any event it remains evidence of the defensive castles that were needed in Castile long after the turbulent Middle Ages had given way to comparative peace elsewhere in Europe. Soon, however, fortresses were being transformed into castles and even palaces, so that for example the fortress built at Cuéllar by the Duke of Albuquerque, Don Bertrán de la Cueva, in the fifteenth century, was given a gothic chapel about a hundred years later and then a renaissance patio.

The religious orders likewise relied on castles and fortresses for self-defence, and often their very churches, such as San Martín at Frómista, are fortified. San Martín is a romanesque church, built in the style brought here in the early eleventh century by Benedictine monks who arrived from France during the reign of Sancho the Great of Navarre. Castles too were built in the romanesque style, such as that which the Knights Templar built in 1178 at Ponferrada and the fortress at Peñafiel. A more delicate, less severe romanesque style appears in many a monastic cloister, particularly that of Santo Domingo de Silos in the province of Burgos.

Nonetheless a remarkable interplay of cultures took place between the Moors and the Christians, leaving its mark on the whole of Castile. Under the Moslems Christians were allowed to practise their religion provided that they paid tribute to their masters. Since the Mozarabs, as these Christians were called, not only dressed as Moors and spoke their language, inevitably they also absorbed Moorish culture. Founded by monks from Córdoba in 913, the monastery of San Miguél de Escalada, east of León, is one of the most entrancing examples of the Mozarab style in Spain.

Till the reign of Ferdinand and Isabella, Christian Spain showed the same tolerance to the conquered Moors. And since the Arabs were the finest builders of the era, their conquerors readily employed them to build new churches. In consequence a unique architectural form arose, known as *mudéjar* from the Arabic *mudayyan*, which means 'the subjected one'. From the twelfth century onwards all the ornamental skills and resources of the Arab world were put to the service of the Christian religion. Decorative brickwork; richly patterned and coffered ceilings known as 'artesonado', often constructed of small pieces of wood and usually painted and gilded; glazed tiles; horseshoe and multi-lobed arches; complex stucco work: these elements combined to produce buildings of heart-stopping beauty. Even the Benedictines, granted privileges at Sahagún, forsook the Romanesque they had brought into Spain and embraced the *mudéjar*. And after Ferdinand and Isabella had expelled the Moors from Spain, the *mudéjar* style lived on to influence the Isabelline Gothic of such palaces as that which in the mid fifteenth century Juan de Guas built for the dukes of Infantado at Manzanares el Real.

Under Christian rule the Moors lived in ghettos, and so did the Jews of Castile. In some cities, particularly León, Burgos and Toledo, their culture flourished. Increasing persecution, popular hatreds fuelled by royal favours granted in exchange for Jewish financial acumen, and the hostility of the Catholic monarchs

---

At Arévalo the twelfth-century church of La Lugareja, whose blind arcades and brick decor form one of the purest ensembles of the *mudéjar* style, once belonged to a Cistercian monastery.

Ferdinand and Isabella led, however, to the eventual expulsion of the Jews from Spain, and even before then to the forcible consecration of their synagogues as Christian churches. Some of these have been restored to their former exquisite state while others remain as permanent memorials to past cruelties. Today the Jewish quarter at Berlanga de Duero is probably the best-preserved in Castile. At Toledo the synagogue was transformed into the church of Santa María la Blanca, while that at Salamanca survives as the church of La Vera Cruz.

Ferdinand II of Aragón (Ferdinand and the Emperor Charles V are the only names anglicized in this book) and Isabella I of Castile, who married in 1479, virtually unified Spain. Known respectively as *el Católico* and *la Católica*, these 'Catholic Kings' inherited a struggle for power between the monarchy and the nobility of Castile which had been raging since the reign of Alfonso X, the Wise, in the thirteenth century. Ferdinand and Isabella therefore issued a decree demanding 'that the ancient castles and fortified rocks and the other fortresses that have been and will be built on our soil in the future be demolished and razed to the ground'. The nobility ignored the decree, though a good number seem to have flattered the sovereigns by having the royal emblems and escutcheon carved on the walls of their castles.

With the discoveries of Christopher Columbus the nation became one of the most powerful in Christendom, its royal emissaries conquering and converting Latin America and enriching the royal treasury with gold. Great cities developed spectacularly. When Isabella died in 1504, her daughter Juana was considered insane and unfit to rule. As her son Carlos was but 4 years old, Ferdinand of Aragón became regent, followed by Cardinal Cisneros. Carlos, who was to be elected Holy Roman Emperor Charles V in 1520, succeeded to the Spanish throne in 1516.

Almost instantly he was faced with the revolt of the Castilian cities, the *comuneros*, organized by members of the nobility and some of the cities. Among the castles which, notwithstanding the order of the Catholic Kings, had remained standing was the fortress at Simancas. Founded by the Moors and partly rebuilt in the Middle Ages, it was embellished sufficiently in the sixteenth century to serve as a jail for prisoners of high rank. Here Charles imprisoned the Bishop of Acuña, who had sided with the *comuneros* in fighting against him. After strangling the governor of the fortress, the bishop was captured as he attempted to escape. A short trial condemned him to death.

This warlike man of God would no doubt have been familiar with the gothic style of architecture, and especially its Flamboyant version which, under the influence of San Juan de los Reyes at Toledo, soon spread throughout Castile. Architects from Cologne added their own skills to Castilian Gothic, above all at Burgos cathedral. In the early sixteenth century it combined with renaissance elements to produce a rich and decoratively complex style that became known as 'plateresque', since it resembled the work of silversmiths (*plateros*). Such plateresque masters as Diego de Siloé, Rodrigo Gil de Hontañón and Alonso de Covarrubias flourished in Castile. At Cogolludo, for instance, some 20 kilometres west of Jadraque, the façade of the Medinaceli palace, which was created in 1595 and whose stones resemble fine-spun lace, is a late example of this style.

For a time, after the abdication of Charles V in 1556 and the succession of Felipe II, a more sombre renaissance style was granted the favour of the court. But the exuberance of Spanish Baroque soon broke out, followed by the theatrically fantastic architectural fashion known as the churrigueresque. This style is named after the architect José de Churriguera (1655–1725) and his brothers Joaquín (1674–1720) and Alberto (1676–1750); the intoxicated creations of his successors, however, went far beyond anything they achieved.

Such fashions could be indulged in only by the wealthy, and the extravagance of these buildings

---

Plateresque fantasy: the façade of the Palacio de Medinaceli at Cogolludo is the work of the architect Lorenzo Vázquez.

The Plaza Mayor at Peñaranda de Duero, with half-timbered houses rising from stone columns, the renaissance Palacio de Avellaneda and the eighteenth-century collegiate church.

ought not to detract from the humbler domestic architecture of the two Castiles. Castilla-La Mancha is a region of whitewashed houses with painted external skirtings. The finer houses often enclose a courtyard with a well. In the mountains houses were often constructed entirely of slate, and many of these, known generically as *arquitectura negra*, are still inhabited, in spite of their often ramshackle appearance. Two-storey houses are common, the upper storey with balconies for drying clothes as much as for sitting, the lower one consisting of a kitchen and living room. Larger farmhouses were built of whitewashed mud and brick, sometimes decorated with ceramics, their two storeys surrounding large inner courtyards overlooked by galleries.

Castilla y León has an even greater variety of domestic architecture, ranging from the rich brown adobe houses of the Tierra de Campos to three-storey farmhouses whose ground-floor living rooms give on to a vegetable garden; on the first floor are the bedrooms, and the upper storey is used for drying and storing. This is a region of lovely half-timbered buildings, often with arcades supported on either wooden or stone pillars.

Castilla-La Mancha is also the home of windmills and is thus haunted by the shade of Don Quixote. Ever since his creation he has continued to fascinate the Spaniards. The twentieth-century philosopher Miguel de Unamuno, who was rector of Salamanca university, when asked what Don Quixote had bequeathed to culture, answered 'Quixotism', adding, 'and that is no little thing. It is a whole method of thought, a whole epistemology, a whole aesthetic, a whole logic, a whole ethic, and above all a whole religion.' Don Quixote, he insisted, represented a complete economy of the eternal and the divine, 'a total hope in what is rationally absurd'.

The celebrated opening of Cervantes's novel takes good care not to identify precisely where his hero was born. 'In a place in La Mancha which I have no desire to name there lived not long ago a gentleman,' begins Sancho Panza, 'one of those men who always have a lance on the rack, an ancient shield, a mangy hack and a greyhound for coursing'. The village of Argamasilla de Alba lays most vehement claim to being at least the place where the Don was mentally conceived. Here you are shown the dungeon in which Cervantes could have been imprisoned (for making a pass at a nobleman's daughter) when he wrote the opening chapters of the novel.

From Argamasilla de Alba runs a so-called *ruta de Don Quijote*. Not far away is El Toboso with its low, lime-washed houses, and certainly Cervantes himself identified this as the spot to which the wondrously half-crazed knight and Sancho crept at around midnight before paying court to the Lady Dulcinea. At least four other towns, Tomelloso, Alcázar de San Juan, Campo de Criptana and Consuegra, claim to be the place where the knight tilted at windmills.

Tomelloso is renowned for its wine as well as its

windmills. Alcázar de San Juan (which incidentally has a partly Mozarabic, partly romanesque church dedicated to Santa María and a museum with Roman mosaics) has named its windmills after characters in *Don Quixote* – including his nag; but it has disqualified itself by displaying for many years a certificate of Cervante's's baptism which was an eighteenth-century fake. Campo di Criptana boasts some thirty windmills, as well as a ruined château and the baroque church of Nuestra Señora de las Angustias (with a fine baroque reredos). It also once belonged to the Knights of Santiago, whose sword appears in the municipal coat of arms. But as the site of the knight's celebrated joust, I plump for Consuegra, if only because its windmills are in decent condition.

This is saffron country, and Consuegra hosts a saffron festival over the last weekend of October. The town's other attractions include the ruins of a Roman circus and aqueduct, and a hilltop castle.

A second Castilian character, this one based on a historical figure but imbued with almost as much fantasy as Don Quixote, is Rodrigo Díaz de Vivar, popularly known as El Cid (from the Arabic for 'lord'). Brought up with the future Sancho II of Castile, when Sancho became king of Castile in 1065 Rodrigo was made his standard-bearer. By now the Moorish unity based on the Caliphate of Córdoba was breaking up, and Sancho, assisted by El Cid, sallied forth against the Moorish stronghold of Zaragoza and made its ruler a fief of Castile.

Rodrigo collaborated with Sancho in attempting to deprive Alfonso VI of the kingdom of León, and when Sancho was killed besieging Zamora, El Cid was beguiled into joining the court of Alfonso. In 1074 he married the king's niece Ximena. But when he attacked the Moorish kingdom of Toledo, at that time dependent on Alfonso for his patronage, El Cid was exiled. He promptly offered his services to the Moors. The king of Zaragoza wisely accepted the aid of a general who had never lost a battle, and during the next decade El Cid on his behalf defeated the Moorish ruler of Lérida and his Christian allies, as well as the army of the Christian king Sancho Ramírez of Aragón.

This fearsome nineteenth-century statue of El Cid stands in the Plaza Primo de Rivera, Burgos.

Reconciled to the Catholic side in 1086, Rodrigo took eight years to conquer Valencia, giving orders when it surrendered for its chief magistrate to be burnt alive. Thenceforth El Cid ruled Valencia virtually as his own private fief, though supposedly on behalf of Alfonso VI. Within a century of his death this brilliant, unscrupulous mercenary had become a Castilian hero, immortalized in the epic poem *El cantar de mío Cid*.

The saffron festival of Consuegra is a reminder that for all its epic traditions Castile is a homely spot and its people live close to the soil. Its gastronomy is homely too. We have it on the word of Sancho that Don Quixote's habitual diet consisted of stew (with more beef than mutton), hash most evenings, lentils on Fridays, boiled bones on Saturdays and as a Sunday treat a young pigeon.

Little has changed. The first important culinary influence on Castile came with the pilgrims who crossed the Pyrenees from France on the way to

23

Santiago de Compostela, and the second was the discovery of America, bringing initially peppers and tomatoes and later the potato. Cereals and pulses from the region's own fields add variety with haricot beans and lentils contributing further refinements. As Sancho Panza once observed, such an *olla podrida* is bound to satisfy: 'With so many ingredients in a stew, I cannot fail to discover something I enjoy.'

Cuchifrito is a slightly more elaborate dish, made from lamb, eggs, tomatoes, kidney beans, saffron and white wine. Spicy pork sausages are almost always on the menu, and much ingenuity is devoted to the cooking of tripe, which seems to me wasted on that hideous offal. Omelettes range from the traditional Spanish variety to those made with crayfish tails from Molina de Aragón. Partridges are widely available, as are a remarkable range of fish from the rivers and lagoons of Castile – a boon during Holy Week when ground cod served with garlic appears on menus as *ajo arriero*. Whereas meals are often finished off with semi-cured cheeses or sponge cake, a traditional Holy Week dessert is *alajú*, a concoction of nuts, honey and bread crumbs.

Fiestas in Castile tend to mix traditional country pastimes with a hint of Castilian passion. They also blend naturally with religious observances. Throughout the region Holy Week is marked by impressive processions in which men, women and children, clad in traditional dress and accompanied by stern music and the beat of drums, carry gruesomely realistic statues depicting the sufferings of Jesus. The beginning of Lent, by contrast, is a gayer affair, when the citizens of Castile light bonfires, dress like South Sea islanders, punchinellos or Benedictine monks and gad about the streets. Corpus Christi is another widely observed festival. Some local fiestas are delightfully weird. At Almonacid del Marquesado on 2 and 3 February (the feast of St Blas) the 'possessed', personified by men in vivid costumes wearing cowbells on

---

An isolated homestead in the landscape south-west of Consuegra.

their backs and flowered head-dresses, invade the streets, finally exchanging their head-dresses for St Blas's mitre and then dancing frenziedly in the parish church.

In such festivals Castilians display both their religious inheritance and their gift for energetic display and boisterous merriment. So long cut off from most of Europe not only by the barrier of the Pyrenees but also by Spain's concentration on her American colonies, this part of the country still presents an often bizarre, sometimes mysterious and always fascinating face to the visitor. As the two Castiles have increasingly opened themselves up to twentieth-century travellers, their peculiar charms have not been destroyed (though around Madrid the need to build cheap apartments has replaced shanty-town squalor with visual blight).

Although many roads are good, and others increasingly improving, the region has for the most part escaped motorways. (If you prefer to take your own car to Castile, the only company sailing regularly from Britain to Spain is Brittany Ferries.) Throughout Spain fine historic buildings have been transformed by the government tourist board into Paradors (a word deriving from *parada*, meaning a stopping place). The very first of these was opened in Castilla y León in 1928 in a hunting lodge in the Gredos mountains. Today it is a centre for summer and winter sports.

These Paradors, along with countless less grand but equally welcoming hotels, inns and small hostels, entice the discerning traveller to use them as bases for exploring the pleasures of these regions. Some of their delights are summed up for me at Almagro, in Castilla-La Mancha in the province of Ciudad Real. The Parador Nacional at Almagro was built as a Franciscan monastery in 1597. The town itself boasts a main square overlooked by blue-painted, balconied windows, shaded by the seventeenth-century church of San Augustin, and the venue for bullfights. If you arrive on 5 August you will discover the faithful celebrating the pilgrimage of the Virgin of the Snows. And all the year round you can relish in the restaurants of Almagro the local speciality: an hors-d'oeuvre of spiced, garlicky aubergines known as *berenkenas*.

25

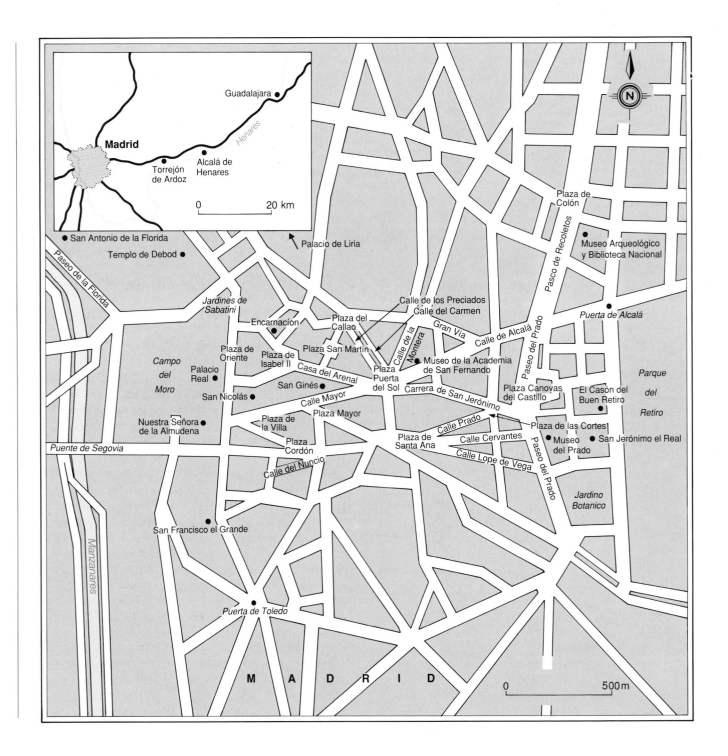

Guadalajara

Madrid

Torrejón
de Ardoz

Alcalá de
Henares

Henares

0   20 km

San Antonio de la Florida

Templo de Debod

Palacio de Liria

Plaza de
Colón

Paseo de la Florida

Jardines de
Sabatini

Encarnacíon

Plaza del
Callao

Calle de los Preciados
Calle del Carmen

Gran Via

Calle de Alcalá

Paseo de Recoletos

Museo Arqueológico
y Biblioteca Nacional

Puerta de Alcalá

Plaza de
Oriente

Plaza de
Isabel II

Casa del Arenal

Plaza San Martín

Calle de la
Montera

Plaza
Puerta
del Sol

Museo de la Academia
de San Fernando

Paseo del Prado

Parque

Campo

del

Moro

Palacio
Real

San Ginés

Carrera de San Jerónimo

Plaza Canovas
del Castillo

El Casón del
Buen Retiro

del

Retiro

San Nicolás

Calle Mayor

Plaza Mayor

Nuestra Señora
de la Almudena

Plaza de
la Villa

Plaza
Cordón

Plaza de
Santa Ana

Calle Prado

Calle Cervantes

Plaza de las Cortes

Museo
del Prado

San Jerónimo el Real

Puente de Segovia

Calle del Nuncio

Calle Lope de Vega

Paseo del Prado

Jardino
Botanico

Manzanares

San Francisco el Grande

Puerta de Toledo

M A D R I D

0   500 m

1
The Capital and its Environs

Madrid – Alcalá de Henares – Guadalajara

To wander along a little alleyway (or *travesía*) in Madrid, to stroll through a narrow street (or *callejón*), to saunter down a flower-bedecked boulevard (or *paseo*), to admire the view from a parapet (or *pretil*), to emerge into one of those garden squares which the Madrileños dub a *jardinillo*, to eat a midday *almuerzo* and to sink into a restaurant in the latish evening for a *cena* is to my mind to savour the delights of a unique Spanish metropolis which, along with a number of other splendid cities described in this book, has never been given its due praise.

To a large extent this is the fault of its own citizens, for they have managed to surround the capital of Spain with some of the most appalling apartment blocks imaginable. Nonetheless, by threading one's way carefully through these horrors it is possible to enjoy the legacy that has been left to us by a far more glamorous past. Enough of it remains to offer a foretaste of the much less despoiled towns and cities which make up the rest of Castile.

Two styles of Spanish architecture dominate Madrid. The first is the *estile Herreriano*. Monumental and austere, it derives its name from the architect Juan de Herrera. Herrera lived from 1530 to 1597, flourishing during the reign of Felipe II, who succeeded to the throne in 1556 when his father, the weary Emperor Charles V, abdicated and retired to a monastery in Extremadura. Herrera's calculatedly mathematical rigour, seen at its finest in the Escorial Monastery and Royal Palace north-west of Madrid, contrasts with the other dominant aspect of the city, its profusely decorated baroque face.

Somehow the stern Herreran style sits better on Madrid, for this is the highest capital in Europe, standing at the centre of vast and arid plains, only the northern horizon enlivened by the peaks of the Sierra de Guadarrama. The climate can be savage, and the Madrilenos have their equivalent to the British proverb 'Ne'er cast a clout till May is out' (*Hasta el cuarenta del Mayo no te quites el sayo*). Once these plains surrounding the city were sheltered by trees, but in the seventeenth and eighteenth centuries the people of Castile felled them, fearing that the birds nesting in them would gobble up their corn. As a result the land, watered only by the rains which fall at the beginning of winter and in April, became yet more parched. In early summer the temperature in Madrid begins to rise spectacularly, and the *madrileños* lock themselves away in the afternoon for the sacred siesta.

Celtic tribes had populated this region during Roman times, to be replaced first by the Visigoths and then by Moslems who, in the mid ninth century under the Emir Mohammed I, fortified a camp here and called it Majerit. Though their mosque and fortress, the

alcázar, have gone, their legacy to the city includes its tortuous ancient streets, a couple of fortified gateways (La Vega and Guadalajara) and its *mudéjar* architecture.

Madrid prospered throughout the Middle Ages. The Catholic Alfonso VI had taken the city in 1083, transforming the Moslem fortress into a Christian one. He and his successors gave the population numerous privileges – in particular the right to hold a fair, which was granted to Madrid in the fifteenth century by Enrique IV of Castile. Carlos I, who came to the throne in 1516 (three years later to become Holy Roman Emperor Charles V) brought here aristocratic families who began building palaces.

It was his son, Felipe II, who in 1561 made Madrid the capital of Spain in place of Valladolid, for he judged that neither Burgos, the favoured city of the Castilians, nor Zaragoza, which was Aragonese, nor the Moorish Seville could unite his country. Felipe chose a city at the geographical heart of Spain. Apart from the court architect Juan de Herrera, it was the seventeenth-century architect Francisco de Mora who set out to transform the city into a worthy capital, and to both Herrera and De Mora we owe the Plaza Mayor, today the hub of Madrid.

In 1701, following the War of the Spanish Succession, Felipe V, the son-in-law of Louis XIV of France, succeeded Carlos II, the last of the Habsburg kings of Spain. Under the Bourbons the city underwent further changes. Madrid has inherited from these years the Toledo bridge, the Paseo de la Florida, the San Vicente gate and two works by the architect Pedro de Ribera, the hospice of San Fernando and the church of San Cayetano. Finally, during the reign of Don Carlos de Bourbon (Carlos III), who renounced the monarchy of Naples to become king of Spain. Madrid was transformed into a city of fountains and glamorous palaces – de Liria, de Villahemosa, de Buenavista and the royal palace itself. Among the most impressive additions to Madrid during his reign, two – the church

---

Madrid baroque: a doorway to the municipal museum by Pedro de Ribera.

of San Francisco el Grande, with its enormous dome, and the Puerta de Alcalá – are the work of his favourite Italian architect, Francisco Sabatini.

From 1808 Spain was ruled for five years by Joseph Bonaparte, who planned to open up the city with new squares and wider roads. Happily he failed, but throughout the nineteenth century spaces were cleared, older squares such as the Plaza Puerta del Sol were enlarged and architects created pastiches of older building styles as well as innovatively using glass and iron. In 1873 the Puente de Segovia, 23 metres high, was thrown across the Río Manzanares, dramatically improving communications. The railways brought a modest increase in the population, which in 1880 was around 400,000, but only under the regime of General Franco did the city (which had resisted him until 28 March 1939) reach anything like its present population: today it has about four million inhabitants. In consequence, though there are wide boulevards such as the Gran Vía, which was opened up in 1907, Madrid remains a blend of spectacular, sometimes Italianate architecture alongside the humbler and charming ancient quarters.

Old Madrid is undoubtedly best visited on foot, starting at the Plaza Puerta del Sol, a hemisphere whose name derives from a gateway which long ago pierced the medieval walls of the city at this point, and which looked towards the rising sun. This particular square is the Rome, so to speak, of Spain, for all roads are said to lead to it and Spanish maps number their distances from here, at kilometres zero. Ten streets of Madrid also home in on this spot. A plaque commemorates the heroes who took on the troops of Napoleon on 2 May 1808; and here in 1931 the Spaniards proclaimed the inauguration of their Second Republic, a socialist regime which was destroyed before the end of the decade by General Franco.

The most impressive building in this square is the neo-classical police headquarters of 1760, whose clock tower dates from a hundred years later. Fashionable boutiques and jewellery shops line Calle de la Montera, Calle del Carmen and Calle de los Preciados, which lead off the Plaza Puerta del Sol to the north. Calle de Alcalá,

running north-east from the square, is more attractive. Lined like the others with boutiques, it also boasts the Museo de la Academia de San Fernando, which in a city stuffed with paintings by Goya has some of his finest portraits. On the left, Casa Real de Adriana displays the influence of eighteenth-century architects on Madrid. Designed by Raffaele Sabatini in 1769, it now serves as the home of the Spanish ministry of financial affairs. The seventeenth-century church of Las Calatravas a little further along the street offers a piquant blend of classical and baroque. Round the corner, just before the church, rises a King-Kong-style skyscraper of 1927 by a genius named López Otero. On the same side of the *calle* is the Madrid casino, an art nouveau jewel of 1910, while on the opposite side is the Banco Española de Credito of 1891, an even more fantastic art nouveau building decorated with swirling ironwork, elephants' heads, an elaborate fantasy of a cupola and bronze hanging lamps.

From the south-west side of the Plaza Puerta del Sol, opposite Calle de Alcalá, runs the Calle Mayor. From it turn immediately left into Calle Esparteros (named after the makers of rush or *esparto* carpets for the court) to reach the Plaza de la Provincia and the Cárcel de Corte, whose name derives from a law court established here by Felipe IV in 1636. Attached to this tribunal was a prison in which for a time the dramatist Lope de Vega was incarcerated. Today the angel-capped brick and stone building, designed by Juan Crescenci in 1634, is the Spanish foreign office.

The Arco de Cuchilleros (the Knife-grinders' Arch) to the west of the square leads to Madrid's glamorous, arcaded Plaza Mayor. Although Juan de Herrera deserves the major honours for designing this square, Felipe III commissioned Juan Gómez de Mora in 1617 to finish the work, and the imprint of his handiwork mostly dominates the square as we see it today – though at the end of the eighteenth century the buildings of the Plaza Mayor had been so much

Belle époque **architecture on the Calle de Terraz, Madrid.**

Felipe III, in bronze, rides majestically through Madrid's Plaza Mayor.

damaged by fire that Juan de Villanueva was employed to rebuild them. He took the opportunity to create at the entrances to the square the arched, offset passageways that are today filled with shops and bars. Finally a bronze equestrian statue of Felipe III, designed by Giambologna and completed by his pupil Pietro Tacca in 1613, was set up at the centre of the square in 1847.

From the west side of the Plaza Mayor, Calle Ciudad Rodrigo takes us on to Calle Cava San Miguel, which is filled with leaning seventeenth-century houses (designed to buttress this side of the main square), inviting *tascas* (or bars) and some fine eating houses. It leads towards the gilded and curvaceous baroque church of San Miguel, which stands in the triangular Plaza Cordón, along with two eighteenth-century palaces and a balconied house of 1852.

From here, by following the narrow Calle Cordón, you reach the quiet, irregular little Plaza de la Villa,

where rises Madrid's triple-towered Casa del Ayuntamiento, or town hall, begun by Juan Gómez de Mora in 1640 and later given a baroque façade. It stands beside the plateresque Casa de Cisneros, which was built in 1537 by Benito Jiménez de Cisneros, nephew of the famous Cardinal Cisneros. Opposite is the Hemeroteca de Madrid, a *mudéjar* building with a gothic balcony and a brick, keyhole-arched doorway. Here too is the Torre de los Lujanes, a sixteenth-century brick and plaster tower in which the French king François I was imprisoned after his capture at the battle of Pavia in 1525. And in the centre of the square is a statue of Alvaro de Bazán with his admiral's baton, set here by the sculptor Gil Mariano Benlliure in 1888.

Where the square adjoins Calle Mayor a wall-plaque announces that here once lived Luis Velez de Guevara, who in 1641 wrote the novel *El diabolo cojuelo*. Walk left down Calle Mayor and on the left you will see the seventeenth-century Iglesia Arcopisbel Castrense, a Maltese cross over its door; inside are frescoes by Antonio González Velázquez and Gregorio Ferro, dating from the eighteenth century.

The architecture of the churches is this corner of Madrid is fascinating. Up an alleyway to the right of the *calle* rises the church of San Nicolás; mentioned in the municipal charter of 1202, it is the oldest in the city, its brick walls filled out with massive stones, its fourteenth-century *mudéjar* brick tower pierced with keyhole lights. On the other side of Calle Mayor rises the façade of the basilica of San Isidro, a cold, baroque masterpiece begun in 1622 by the Jesuits to provide a worthy shrine for the body of St Isidro. The newly canonized saint had been born in Madrid in 1070 and worked all his life as a labourer on the estate of a wealthy farmer just outside the city. Isidro died on 15 May 1130. Even in his lifetime he and his wife María Torribia were noted for their devout Christian ways, and after their deaths more and more miracles were

performed for those who prayed to them. Though Isidro was long regarded as a saint (as was María), it was when intercessions to him cured Felipe III of a serious illness that the king set in motion the appeal for his official canonization. Now Madrid celebrates his feast from 10–26 May, with bullfights nearly every day; whether you seek this out is a matter of taste.

Further south from San Isidro stands San Cayetano, another baroque church, its façade of 1722 designed by Pedro de Ribera, the rest the work of José de Churriguera. This ancient quarter of Madrid is celebrated for its sprawling Sunday flea-market which centres on the Plaza del Rastro and stretches as far as the Puerta de Toledo.

West of San Isidro, in the Calle del Nuncio, is the church of San Pedro, with its fifteenth-century *mudéjar* tower, and further west still is another baroque delight, San Andrés. To the north-west of this church stands the gleaming white Palacio Real, in Madrid's largest square, the Plaza de Oriente, beside the Catedral de la Almudena. In the centre of the square is a bronze equestrian statue of Felipe IV by Pietro Tacca dating from 1640. The local guides tell you that the rearing horse maintains its equilibrium because its tail is filled with lead. The complex sculpting of the tail is matched by the intricacies of the mane and Felipe's cloak. In the reliefs on one side of the base his queen encourages charity and the arts and sciences, while on the other Felipe decorates Velázquez with the cross of Santiago. Surrounding the monument are marble statues of Visigothic and Spanish rulers. And across the square from the royal palace is Madrid's mid nineteenth-century Teatro Real, inaugurated in 1850 with Donizetti's *La favorita*.

The Palacio Real is vast and spectacular. When the medieval *alcázar* which overlooked the River Manzanares burned down in 1724, Felipe V, true to the Italianate taste of the time, called upon the Sicilian architect Filippo Juvarra to replace it. Juvarra designed a palace a kilometre in length. Alarmed at the expense of such a grandiose project, the king commissioned another Italian, Giovanni Battista Sacchetti, to design something more manageable. Begun in 1738,

In the Plaza de Oriente, Madrid, the bronze charger of Felipe IV, founded in Florence in 1640, rears spectacularly.

33

the classical palace, built of granite with facings in marble, was given a couple of wings to create the present harmoniously proportioned courtyard known as the Plaza de la Armería, which overlooks a garden (the Campo del Moro) sloping down to the river. Laid out in 1844, this garden was embellished a year later by a Triton fountain which came from Aranjuez. To the north of the palace is another exquisite Madrid park, the Jardines de Sabatini, covering 21,000 square metres, with a lush fountain amid its box parterres, and a bronze statue of Carlos III overlooking its marble statuary. A few paces east rises the convent of the Encarnación, which Queen Margarita, wife of Felipe III, commissioned in 1611 from Juan Gómez de Mora. Today it is a museum and art gallery. Calle Serrano Suner runs by it, leading to the senatorial palace, a fifteenth-century building created for Augustinian monks, and to the Grimaldi palace, which was built by Sabatini in 1776.

But the royal palace is the star attraction. Among the Italian artists who decorated its interior was the baroque master Giovanni Battista Tiepolo. The magnificent marble staircase has a vaulted ceiling painted by Corrado Giaquinto showing the Spanish sovereign paying homage to religion. Napoleon Bonaparte is reputed to have told his brother Joseph, temporarily ruler of Spain, 'Here you have finer lodgings than mine'. Antonio González Velázquez painted the ceiling of Queen Cristina's antechamber and Tiepolo decorated the vault of the throne room, depicting in baroque grandeur the kingdom of Spain and its dependencies. The throne itself is guarded by two gilded bronze lions. Tiepolo was also responsible for decorating the ceiling of the hall of the halberdiers. For Carlos III's study he painted St Peter of Alcántara. The palace also houses works by such masters as Rubens, Goya, Watteau and of course Velázquez, some fine tapestries, collections of glass and porcelain and a library of 300,000 books.

Steps rise from the winter garden to Madrid's colossal Palacio Real.

After the magnificence of the royal palace, the cathedral of Nuestra Señora de la Almudena promises more than it delivers. 'Almudena' derives from the Moorish word for 'corn store', and the building we see here today stands on the site of a Moslem mosque converted into a church by Alfonso VI in the eleventh century. This was previously the oldest church in Madrid. The present cathedral was built in the nineteenth and twentieth centuries (and work is not yet complete). Its towers are renaissance in style, and its classical façade conceals an excellent gothic-style interior designed by Francisco de Cubas in 1880. The crypt is nineteenth-century romanesque. As John Harvey put it in his *Cathedrals of Spain*, 'There is a faintly ridiculous side to this historical pageantry of painstaking copies of the national styles adopted in succession for the various sections of the work but at least Madrid, the artificial capital of an artificial grouping of kingdoms, is being provided with an artificial epitome of all the cathedrals of Spain.'

Far more impressive, a little way further south, is the majestic basilica of San Francisco el Grande, Spain's pantheon. The Franciscans built this church in the twelfth century and entirely rebuilt it in the eighteenth, surmounting the austere classical pile with one of the largest domes in the world (its diameter is 33 metres) and creating a plausible imitation of the Pantheon in Rome.

Of its seven chapels, four contain huge and fascinating altar paintings, all of them illuminated by openings in the ceiling. The first on the left, the plateresque chapel of San Bernardino of Siena, has a painting by El Greco depicting the saint preaching to a group of knights. Francisco de Zurbarán contributed a portrait of the Franciscan monk St Bonaventure in the adjoining chapel, which is built in the Byzantine style. For the Spanish renaissance chapel of Carlos III, Agosto Plasencia painted the king in a gorgeous blue velvet cloak kneeling before the Virgin of the Immaculate Conception. In the next chapel, dedicated to the military orders of Spain, is a painting by José Casado del Alisál of St James the Great on a white charger, vigorously slaying Moors at the battle of Clavijo.

Casado del Alisál was responsible for another painting in the same chapel, this one depicting crusaders laying their arms before the Pope before departing for the Holy Land. The sacristy's chief treasure is a set of Spanish renaissance stalls which once graced the monastery of El Paular, to the north of Madrid, while among the paintings in the cloisters are four more saints by Zurbarán.

To the north of San Francisco el Grande are two oddities. First, in the Jardines de la Montaña del Príncipe Pío, is an Egyptian temple. The fourth-century BC Templo de Debod was transferred from the Nile to Spain by the Egyptians in 1970 in gratitude for Spanish help in saving the Nubian Valley. And along the Paseo de la Florida, which stretches beside the garden, is the hermitage of San Antonio de la Florida. Built in 1798 by the Italian architect Francesco Fontana, its dome and transepts were frescoed by Goya, whose body lies here (though by the time it came to be transferred from Bordeaux, where he died, it had mysteriously lost its head).

To the east is the Plaza de Isabel II, with its statue of the queen herself. Casa del Arenal leads south-east from here past the Mozarabic church of San Ginés. First built in 1624 and rebuilt after a fire in 1872, it houses a painting by El Greco of Jesus driving the money-changers from the Temple of Jerusalem. Just before San Ginés, Calle Postigo San Martín runs left to the Plaza San Martín, in which stands the Convento de las Descalzas Reales, a former royal palace. The convent was founded for the Poor Clares in 1559 by the Infanta Joan of Austria, daughter of the Emperor Charles V, who as a young widow longed to retire from worldly affairs.

Here, from 1596 till his death in 1611, lived as director of music one of the finest composers of polyphonic religious music of the era. Tomás Luis de Victoria had studied in Rome and succeeded Palestrina

as the Maestro di Capella of the Collegium Romanum. Ordained priest, he became chaplain to the sister of Felipe II, who brought him back with her to Spain and took him into the convent of the Descalzas Reales when she herself retired there.

The first architects of this remarkable convent were Juan Bautista de Toledo and Antonio Sillero. Juan Gómez de Mora added his indelible imprint in the seventeenth century. Since the convent attracted numerous royal princesses and widows, it also attracted lavish donations. Today it houses a collection of gold and liturgical objects, together with superb tapestries commissioned by Isabella of Austria from Rubens and paintings in which he depicted the triumph of the Catholic Church over heresy. Here too are works by Peter Breughel the Elder, a portrait of St Francis of Assisi by Zurburán and Titian's scornful depiction of Jesus and the Tribute Money.

Walking north from the convent to the Plaza del Callao (whose Telefónica of 1929 was once the highest building in Spain), take the usually crowded Gran Vía to the right in order to reach the Plaza de la Cibeles. In the centre of the square is a fountain depicting Cybele enthroned in a chariot drawn by a pair of lions symbolizing harmony and elegance. This celebrated sculpture was created in the eighteenth century by Francisco Gutiérrez and Roberto Michel. South of the square is the Casa de Correos, a secular art nouveau temple dedicated to the notion of progress and designed in 1898. Opposite is another monumental late nineteenth-century building, the Banco de España, whose treasures include five rarely exhibited Goyas.

Two elegant avenues run from this plaza. The Paseo de Recoletos leads northwards towards the Plaza de Colón, with its statue of Christopher Columbus and, just off to the right, the Museo Arqueológico Nacional, the most important museum in Madrid after the Prado, with collections ranging from prehistoric times to the nineteenth century. Housed in the same building is the Biblioteca Nacional, which has 800 different editions of Cervantes's *Don Quixote*. The Paseo del Prado leads south from Plaza de la Cibeles by way of Plaza Canovas del Castillo, where a statue of Neptune sits at the centre

Reflected in a lake, the Egyptian Temple of Debod unexpectedly rises above the Paseo del Pintor Rosales in Madrid's Parque del Oeste.

of a fountain in a curious paddle-wheeled chariot drawn by sea horses. It was sculpted by Juan Pascal de Mena in 1780. The Ritz and the Palace hotels are by contrast much younger creations, dating respectively from 1910 and 1912. Both with corner cupolas, they have aged wonderfully well.

Before walking on to the Prado, make a little literary diversion westwards from the Palace Hotel along the Carrera de San Jerónimo. A few paces take you as far as the Plaza de las Cortes, under whose trees stands the first Spanish statue which was neither regal nor mythological. Set up in 1835, its subject is Cervantes (in full, for the first and last time, Miguel de Cervantes Saavedra). On one side of its plinth the scrawny knight is accompanied by an angel and a pensive Sancho Panza, and on the other a sleepy-looking lion is let out of its cage. In this episode from *Don Quixote*, the crack-brained knight wants to fight the lion and has forced the reluctant carter to let the beast out. Equally inevitably the lion has no interest in fighting. After a leisurely yawn the noble beast licks the dust out of his eyes, washes his face, presents his hindquarters to the knight and calmly goes back into his cage. At this Don Quixote orders Sancho to give the carter two crowns, and decides he shall thenceforth exchange his sobriquet 'the knight of the sad countenance' for the title 'the knight of the lions'.

Calle Prado runs from here to the Plaza de Santa Ana, for which Juan de Villanueva sculpted the statue of the great seventeenth-century Spanish dramatist Calderón (in full, Pedro Calderón de la Barca) who faces the modern Teatro Español. Around the corner in Calle de Nuñez de Arce is a building covered in superb ceramics made in 1928 by Alfonso Romero and depicting Madrid and other great cities of Spain.

This part of Madrid is crammed with baroque palaces, art nouveau buildings, little bars and hotels, overhanging balconies and, fittingly, theatres, for just

Neptune arrogantly rides a giant snail drawn by two sea-horses in Plaza Canovas del Castillo.

south-east of the Plaza de Santa Ana, Calle Cervantes runs back towards the Prado, past the house which Lope de Vega bought in 1610. In the parallel *calle* to the south, which is named after him, is the baroque convent of Las Trinitarias Descalzas, in whose church Cervantes was buried in 1616. His daughter became a nun here and the daughter of Lope de Vega the abbess.

Calle Lope de Vega leads us all the way to the Prado. Undoubtedly Madrid's greatest attraction, this classical palace was built by Juan de Villanueva in the second half of the eighteenth century for King Carlos III. Utilized as an arsenal during the Napoleonic Wars, it suffered grievously, but its essential grandeur remains. Villanueva employed the Doric order of architecture for his main entrance, switching to the Ionic for the galleries and the northern entrance and the Corinthian for the south façade.

Its galleries house the prodigious art collection of the Spanish royal family. Romanesque art shades into the

An eighteenth-century fountain of Cybele, the goddess of plenty, installed in the Plaza de la Cibeles at the behest of King Carlos III.

Gothic. And renaissance paintings lead on to the work of Doménikos Theotokópoulos, who came to Spain in 1577 and is universally known as El Greco. (One of his pictures on display here, the *Adoration of the Shepherds*, El Greco intended for the chapel in which he wished to be buried.) Masterpieces by José de Ribera, Murillo (fifty canvases), Goya, Coello and Velázquez are set beside the works of Italians such as Fra Angelico, Botticelli, Titian (some forty of them), Raphael and Caravaggio. Among Tintoretto's works is a lovely painting of Jesus washing the feet of his disciples. In other rooms hang paintings by such Flemish geniuses as Hieronymus Bosch, Rubens (more than seventy works), Van Dyck and Jacob Jordaens. Among the Germans are Hans Baldung Grien and Dürer, and among the French Claude and Poussin.

The works of Velázquez and Goya form the heart of the collection. Diego Rodríguez da Silva y Velázquez was born in Seville in the last year of the sixteenth century and died in Madrid 61 years later. At the age of 24 he was invited by a fellow Sevillian, Count Gaspar de Guzmán Olivares, chief minister of Felipe IV, to paint his master's portrait. Sadly the work has been lost, but we know that the 18-year-old king was so captivated by it that he made the artist one of his court painters and announced that no-one else should ever paint his portrait.

Velázquez relished the Titians in the royal collection. He befriended Rubens who visited Madrid in 1628, and under the influence of the Flemish artist spent three years in Italy, studying especially the great Venetian painters. He returned to take up Felipe's commission to paint one of the greatest works now on display in the Prado: *The Surrender of Breda*, in which the victorious Spanish commander Ambroglio Spinola receives – with immense courtesy – the keys of the city from the conquered Justin of Nassau.

As a portrait painter Velázquez is superbly represented in the Prado, his humanity shining particularly through the paintings of the court dwarfs, many of whom were artifically stunted as children by being fed knotweed. His most complex painting, *Las Meninas* ('The Maids of Honour') also hangs here. Velázquez himself appears in it by his easel, working on a joint portrait of the king and queen, who are reflected in a looking glass. Other members of the royal family are grouped in his studio, and the Infanta Margarita and her maids of honour have just entered the room. Finally the painting pays tribute to Rubens by including in the background two of his paintings, depicting the disgrace of human beings who presume to challenge the gods.

Francisco José de Goya y Lucientes was born in 1746, the son of an Aragonese master gilder. In the mid 1770s he was in Madrid making cartoons for the royal tapestries, 63 of which are displayed in the Prado. Carlos IV made him a court painter in 1789. When he became principal court painter ten years later he contributed the remarkably honest portrait of the royal family which hangs here.

By now he had been seriously ill and was completely deaf. He had also developed a scandalous relationship with the Duchess of Alba, a widow who was probably the subject of two paintings that were considered so erotic that Goya was chastized by the Inquisition. The inquisitor wrote that 'one of them represents a naked woman on a bed and the other a woman, also on a bed and clothed as a *maya*'.

A *maja* is an Andalusian gypsy, but at carnival time aristocratic Spanish women would don *maja* costume, often as a sign that they would remove it for the right suitor. In Goya's painting the clothed woman is clearly such an aristocractic woman, for her bedding is sumptuously trimmed with lace, while her slippers and her black bolero jacket are edged with gold.

The Duchess of Alba already possessed an erotic painting by Velázquez, the *Toilet of Venus*, which now hangs in the National Gallery in London. Scholars suggest that Goya may have painted her nude when he visited her Andalusian villa, Sanlúcar, in 1797. Others point out that the head of the naked *maja* sits oddly on her body, suggesting perhaps that the nude body is not

This bronze statue of Velázquez stands in front of the Prado.

hers but that of another woman – possibly one of the duchess's servants.

The recently widowed duchess was 34 and Goya was 50 when they became lovers. A portrait of her from this time, dressed in a black *maja* costume, hangs in Madrid's Biblioteca Nacional. One of her rings is engraved 'Alba' and another 'Goya', while she points to the ground where she has traced with her shoe the words 'Solo Goya'. In the same gallery hang other, quite extraordinary, contemporary pictures by Goya done in brush and grey wash. One depicts one of the duchess's servant girls, naked in front of a mirror, her back towards us, a clear reference to Velázquez's *Toilet of Venus*. Another brush and wash drawing is of the duchess herself, standing and facing the spectator. She is fully clothed, but on the recto of the same sheet her back is towards us and she looks coquettishly over her shoulder at the viewer, her skirts raised to display her naked legs and buttocks.

In 1802 this remarkable woman unexpectedly died, leaving an annuity for Goya's son. Two years earlier, for an as yet unexplained reason, she had given both the naked *maja* and her *Toilet of Venus* to an adventurer, Don Manuel Godoy. Though eventually disgraced, he had risen to political power, partly through a liaison with the wife of Carlos III, Queen María Luisa. Goya evidently detested him, and has left us a sketch in which a donkey is seen scrutinizing Godoy's family tree. But by 1880 Godoy had acquired the house in which Goya lived, and when the politician asked him to paint a clothed *maja* to set alongside the naked one he readily complied.

Even when Joseph Bonaparte became king of Spain Goya managed to remain chief court painter. From this time date his savage *Disasters of War*, which nightmarishly portray the inhumanity of both Spanish and French troops. He became a Spanish patriot again with the restoration of Ferdinando VII, painting two splendidly patriotic scenes depicting the citizens of Madrid rising up against the French in 1808, which now hang in the Prado.

Soon sickness forced him into virtual retirement in the 'House of the Deaf Man' just outside Madrid. Here, in the early 1820s, he executed a series of ferociously disturbing works using blacks, greys and browns. Many of these so-called 'black paintings' hang today in the Prado, among them probably the most celebrated, *Satan Devouring his Own Sons*. In 1824 Ferdinando VII allowed the sick man to leave Spain in order to try to regain his health in Bordeaux, but there, four years later, he died.

A nearby annex to the Prado, El Casón del Buen Retiro, houses nineteenth- and twentieth-century Spanish paintings and a collection bequeathed to Madrid by Pablo Picasso. The Casón (designed by Ricardo Velázquez Bosco in the 1880s) stands just beyond the church of San Jerónimo el Reál (which has Madrid's only medieval gothic nave). Picasso's most celebrated work in this gallery is the savage *Guernica*, representing the carnage caused by Nazi planes on 26 April 1937, when they bombed the Basque village of the same name, an air raid which cost 1600 Spanish lives. Refusing to allow the work into Spain until democracy was restored to his native land, Picasso lent it to the Museum of Modern Art in New York, and *Guernica* reached the Prado only in 1981.

To the south of the Prado is Madrid's Botanic Garden, laid out in 1781 by Juan de Villanueva for Carlos III though considerably replanted since then. And east of the Prado is the city's favourite park, the Parque del Retiro, first laid out in the fifteenth century around an artificial lake. It once belonged to a monastery, and to its palace the Spanish royal family would retire when in mourning.

The road north-east from Madrid is decidedly drab, yet I advise you to take it to seek out two spots whose treasures, hidden as they are among modern housing blocks, are worth half a day of anyone's time. Thirty-three kilometres east of Madrid stands the birthplace of Miguel de Cervantes. (On the way to it, if you have

A whimsical-looking statue of Miguel de Cervantes stands in Alcalá de Henares, where he was born in 1547.

time, call at Torrejón de Ardoz whose baroque church houses a Martyrdom of St John the Baptist by Coello.)

A classical arch pierces the remains of the fourteenth-century *mudéjar* walls at Alcalá de Henares, where Cervantes, the fourth son of a surgeon, was born. He led a life more eventful than that of most authors. Having lost a hand at the battle of Lepanto in 1571, he was later taken captive by the Turks and spent five years as a prisoner in Algiers. Four times he tried, and failed, to escape. His freedom was finally bought by his family and some Trinitarian monks.

On his return to Spain Cervantes settled in Madrid, married, fathered an illegitimate daughter, and wrote nearly thirty ephemeral plays. Finding work as a tax collector for the kingdom of Granada, he was imprisoned for a while for spending the money instead of handing it over to his employers. Finally he achieved fame and the envy of his fellow author Lope de Vega with the publication of part one of *Don Quixote* in 1605. Cervantes's public longed for the appearance of the second part, but the author's muse directed him instead to write some less successful – though many critics, myself not included, consider equally brilliant – short novels. Only when an anonymous rival brought out a fake second section of his greatest work was Cervantes prompted to produce the authentic sequel. As the last chapter prudently observes upon the noble knight's death, 'When the priest perceived that he was no more, he instructed the clerk to draw up a certificate stating that Alonso Quixote the good, commonly known as Don Quixote de la Mancha, had left this present world and died a natural death, which witness he needed to prevent any author save Cide Hamete Benegeli from falsely bringing him back to life and inventing interminable anecdotes of his acts.' As for Cervantes, like many an author, he died poor.

In the arcaded Calle Mayor is a Cervantes museum and library and in the Plaza Cervantes his statue; but

---

The plateresque façade of the university of Alcalá de Henares, designed by Rodrigo Gil de Hontañón, is topped by an italianate colonnade.

the true fame of Alcalá de Henares derives not so much from Cervantes as from the desire of the Catholic Kings, Ferdinand and Isabella, to espouse the Spanish Counter-Reformation, which was being enthusiastically promoted by the Primate of Spain, Cardinal-Archbishop Francisco Ximénez de Cisneros of Toledo. They lent their prestige to the foundation in 1495 of a new Catholic university here, and paid for most of it. Even before the first lecture was given (in 1508) the town was making an indelible mark on theological studies, for in 1502, to mark the birth of the future Emperor Charles V, Cisneros published at Alcalá a superbly printed edition of the Bible which contained the Old Testament text in Greek, Latin and Hebrew and the New Testament in Greek and Latin. Known as the 'Complutensian Polyglot', this marvellous piece of Catholic scholarship had its thunder stolen simply because it was not circulated throughout the Christian world until 1522, whereas the humanist Erasmus managed to put out his own Greek Bible in 1516.

'Complutensian' derives from Compludo, the name of a monastery founded on a Roman site just across the river from Alcalá in the mid seventh century, and which itself derives from the Roman Complutum. The present name of the town is a legacy of the Moors, who built a fortress where Alcalá de Henares now rises and called it Al-Kala-en-Nahr ('the castle'). But Cisneros brought the place to its apogee in terms of scholarly significance and architectural splendour. It soon began to extend outwards from the university, and its intellectual reputation brought the cream of the religious orders here. Today there are guided tours around the university and two superb patios, or courtyards, of the original university building, the earlier built in 1557 by Pedro de la Cotera, the later in 1676, its three storeys decorated with the Cisneros swans and the coat of arms of Santo Tomé de Villanueva. Visitors can also see the great hall where students long ago were examined for their degrees. The richness of the coffered and painted artesonado ceiling in this hall is matched by the plateresque reading desks and galleries. On the splendid façade of the college, also plateresque, which Rodrigo Gil de

The captivating patio of the Palacio de los Duques del Infantado at Guadalajara, a blend of flamboyant gothic and *mudéjar* architecture.

Hontañón designed in 1526, Cardinal Cisneros had incised the swan of his coat of arms, and also the cord of the Franciscans; renouncing his immense wealth, the cardinal had entered the Franciscan order in 1482 and followed a personal regime of extreme austerity. He lies, in a somewhat damaged marble tomb by Bartolomé Ordóñez, in the richly decorated *mudéjar* Capilla de San Ildefonso, the university chapel.

Oddly enough, no-one has canonized Cisneros or made him patron saint of Alcalá de Henares. That honour is reserved to two fourth-century infant martyrs who now lie in the fifteenth-century gothic Iglesia Magistral in Calle de Empacinado, which runs off Calle Mayor. Their protection has not been universally effective, however. In the thirteenth century the archbishops built at Alcalá de Henares a fortified palace which proved unable to resist the bombardments of the Spanish Civil War. Some of it remains,

including the façade and patios built by Alonso de Covarrubias around 1530.

Twenty-five kilometres further north-east, Guadalajara rises on an eminence to the right of the main road. Faced with the depressing brick and concrete of its suburbs, I must confess that I have often been tempted to retreat to one of the workmen's restaurants in the side streets for some meat balls (*albendigas*) and *patatas fritas*, followed by the sweet sponge cake (*bizcocho borracho*) of the town, the whole washed down with a Vino Blanco Seco Valdepeñas; but one should persist. As the partly rebuilt Roman bridge over the Río Henares reveals, this is a Roman foundation, and when the Moors occupied the site they considerably enlarged and enhanced it, giving it the name Guad al Hadjar, which means stony river. El Cid's ally, Alvar Fañes, re-took Guadalajara on behalf of the Catholics, and soon the town was a stronghold of the Mendoza family.

Built in the 1480s and bombed during the Spanish Civil War, the Palacio de los Duques del Infantado, in Plazo de los Caidos, has retained only its beautiful façade and a patio enclosed by swirling columns, the elaborate spandrels of the two-tier arcading carved with the griffins and eagles of the Mendoza escutcheons. Juan and Enrique de Guas built the palace for Iñigo de Mendoza, second duke of Infantado. The very loveliness of the façade, studded with stones faceted like diamonds, above which rises a gothic and *mudéjar* loggia with little round balconies and slender pillars, makes one deeply regret what has been lost.

Today the palace serves as the town museum, displaying objects from antiquity and gothic tombs. From the Plaza de los Caidos, Calle Teniente Figueroa leads to the church of Santiago, with its coffered ceiling, its *mudéjar* frieze and the plateresque chapel which Alonso de Covarrubias built as the family vault of the Zúñigas. Opposite, beside a renaissance palace which once belonged to Antonio de Mendoza, is the

Part of the powerful medieval fortress of Manzanares el Real.

convent of La Piedád, which was founded by a daughter of the Duke of Infantado. Not far away is the sixteenth-century church of San Miguel, almost adjoining which is the Moorish Luís de Lucena chapel of 1540. Again its brick decorations display typical *mudéjar* delicacy. Moorish elements appear in the horseshoe arches and tower of the brick-built church of Santa María de la Fuente – not surprisingly since this church was once a mosque. Lastly, the church of San Francisco, once part of a thirteenth-century hospice of the Knights Templars, now serves as the mausoleum of the dukes of Infantado.

Since Guadalajara has suffered the same modern building blight as the capital, *madrileños* at weekends prefer to escape their city not to here but north-west along the 607 towards the slopes of the Sierra de Guadarrama, and above all to Manzanares el Real. The village, which lies beside an artificial lake (the barrage of Santillana) is a base for excursions and rock-climbing in the massif of Pedriza. Its early sixteenth-century parish church of Nuestra Señora de las Nieves has a gothic spire and north porch as well as renaissance capitals and a renaissance reredos.

Rising above the village and lending an inimitable allure to the region is the castle which Iñigo López de Mendoza, poet and Count of Santillana, began building in 1435 around a thirteenth-century hermitage. His son, Hurtado de Mendoza, first Duke of Infantado, set about transforming the fortress into a palace, and the 2nd Duke brought Juan de Guas, the celebrated architect of San Juan de Los Reyes at Toledo, to incorporate his own exquisite gothic-*mudéjar* decorations into the building. Guas added double machicolations, turning the castle into a superb pastiche of a medieval fortress. To accentuate its martial aspect he incorporated stone pseudo-cannonballs in the outer walls of the tower. A lower outer wall mimics the battlements and turrets rising above it. Beautifully restored in 1960, the castle at Manzanares el Real has been taken over and furnished by the community of Madrid, is open to the public and is an entrancing venue for conferences, seminars and festivals.

The Río Lozoya flows through the lush Sierra de Guadarrama.

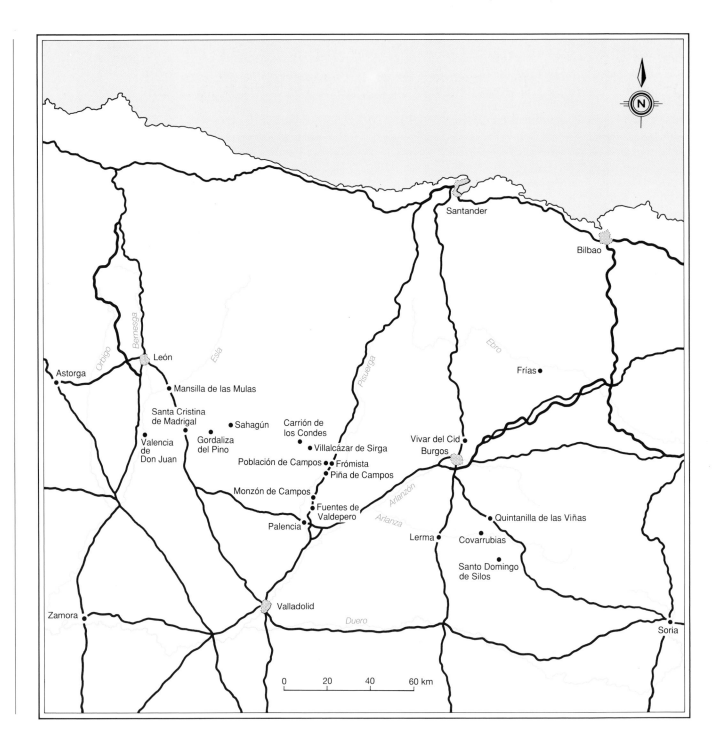

2
From Burgos to Astorga
Burgos – Palencia – Léon – Astorga

Situated beside the Río Arlanzón, Burgos is a far younger city than most of the ancient foundations of Castile. Yet it is as redolent of Spanish history as any of them, the centre of the adventures and triumphs of Rodrigo Díaz de Vivar, the legendary El Cid. Born in 1043 in the dusty village of Vivar del Cid, 9 kilometres north of Burgos, El Cid is celebrated in the oldest Spanish *chanson de geste* to have survived, the twelfth-century *El cantar de mío Cid*, long preserved in the Franciscan convent of his native village.

The ruined *castillo* of the city is also redolent of the hero. You drive straight up to it if you penetrate the walls of Burgos by way of the fourteenth-century Moorish Arco de San Martín. The castle is a reminder of why Burgos was founded, by a certain Diego Porcelos in the 880s; he was bidden to build it by Alfonso III who needed a strategic fortress to resist the advances of the Muslims. By popular tradition a metal bar set in its vault is exactly the length of El Cid's sword, Tizona.

On the way to the castle you pass the imposing eighteenth-century Seminario Mayor de San Jerónimo, built on the site of El Cid's family home. Today you need a good deal of imagination to visualize the house in which he lived, for the 'solar del Cid' now consists of nothing more than a stele and a couple of obelisks marking the spot where it stood till its demolition in

1771. Beyond it is the Arco de Fernán González, a graceful classical archway erected in 1592 by Felipe II in honour of the first count of Castile, who died in 970. Then, as you climb to explore the *castillo*, spare a glance at the church of San Esteban and at the ramparts and arch nearby. The early gothic chuch dates from 1280 to 1350. Over the tympanum is a relief of the Last Supper, and above a balustrade an elaborate rose window lightens the grim aspect of the belfry. Inside, a plateresque chapel in the right-hand aisle contains two fine tombs, that of María de Ortiz de la Costana who died in 1505 and that of Rodrigo de Frías who died in 1510. Its relief depicts the Scourging of Jesus. On the other side of the church a renaissance recess contains another tomb, that of Don Pedro Lupi Gomiel, this time with another relief of the Last Supper. The little cloister attached to the church dates from the fourteenth century. The *mudéjar* horsehoe arch of San Esteban, protected by two square towers and a gallery of six brick arches, was built a century earlier.

This part of Burgos is a quarter of steep, worn steps and charming, ancient crannies. A short way to the east along Calle de Fernán González the sixteenth-century arch of San Gil leads through to the late thirteenth-century church of San Gil, which is crammed with gothic and plateresque tombs and reredoses, the finest to my mind the plateresque

reredos of the Capilla de la Natividad, almost matched in richness by a gothic reredos of the three wise men.

The *castillo*, fortress-home of the early kings, has been severely treated by history. Much disappeared in a conflagration of 1736. Worse was yet to come. In 1812 the Duke of Wellington besieged Burgos and was driven off by the French, but their position proved increasingly untenable, and when they retreated in June the following year they blew up most of the fortress. Now enclosed in a public park, its rugged site still offers a panorama of the city, looking down on Spain's finest gothic cathedral, third only in size to those of Seville and Toledo.

On the way back to the cathedral you pass the early fifteenth-century gothic church of San Nicolás. Francisco de Colonia sculpted its superb reredos, with no fewer than 465 figures depicting scenes from the life of the patron saint and stories from the Old and New Testaments, as well as a representation of the Virgin Mary. On the left-hand side of the high altar are the early sixteenth-century tombs of Gonzalo Polanco and his wife, while Alfonso Polanco, who died in 1490, lies with his wife on the other side of the altar.

Fretted and glistening white, the twin spires of Burgos cathedral match the eight crocketed spires of its lantern. The first stone of the building was laid in 1221 by an English Bishop of Burgos, and the high altar was consecrated seven years later. Another three centuries were to pass before the cathedral was finished. Three doorways pierce the 84-metres-high façade. Although many of the carvings of this west front have been mutilated over the centuries, the reliefs of the Conception and the Assumption, both the work of Juan de Poves in 1653, on the two side portals remain intact and entrancing. Piercing this façade is a magnificent rose window, with a Flamboyant balcony below it and, above, a frieze of statues whose slender height gives them a human scale when seen from far below. The spires were built by Juan de Colonia in the fifteenth

Part of the Puerta del Sarmental of Burgos cathedral, showing a soaring St John and a desk-bound St Matthew with five more of the apostles beneath them.

century, their fretted stonework open to the clear light of the skies, a staircase tower adding its bulk to the right-hand one. Juan de Colonia, father of Francisco came from Cologne, and this accounts for the German late gothic appearance of the spires.

You enter the cathedral on the south side, by the thirteenth-century French gothic Puerta del Sarmental. Its sculptures are in superb condition, with Jesus enthroned between his four evangelists above a frieze of the twelve apostles. Inside is a spacious church whose length, from the west end of the enclosed choir to the Puerta Principal, is precisely the same as the height of the west façade. The nave and two aisles are almost exactly bisected by the transept in which we find ourselves.

The extraordinarily delicate lantern rises to a height of 50 metres over the crossing between the choir and

The main façade of Burgos cathedral, whose magnificent twin spires rise to 84 metres.

These enclosed balconies add charm to the cathedral quarter of Burgos.

the Capilla Mayor (or sanctuary). Its design is the work of Philip of Burgundy, and it was finished in 1567 by his colleagues Juan de Vallejo and Juan de Castañeda. Alongside the escutcheon of the city of Burgos, its decoration includes the arms of the Emperor Charles V. Here too are depicted seraphim, prophets and patriarchs. Beneath the lantern is the tomb of El Cid and his wife Ximena, whose father was Count Díaz de Oviedo. Rodrigo Díaz de Vivar had not wished to be buried here, firmly instructing in his will *A San Pedro de Cardeña mando que mi cuerpo lleven* ('I order that my body be taken to San Pedro de Cardeña'). Initially his corpse did lie in the church of San Pedro, about 9 kilometres outside the city, but after wandering a while (as far as Sigmaringen in Germany), it finally came to rest here.

The choir, built between 1497 and 1512 and protected by a superb grille of 1602, fittingly houses the enamelled bronze tomb of Bishop Mauricio, the man who laid the foundation stone of this cathedral. Lining the side walls are walnut choir stalls, designed by Felipe Vigarni and carved with scenes from the Old Testament and classsical mythology.

On the other side of the tomb of Spain's greatest warrior, El Cid, is the Capilla Mayor whose renaissance reredos was carved in the second half of the sixteenth century by four different hands: Rodrigo and Martín de la Haya, Domingo de Berriz and Juan de Anchieta. The eighteenth-century trascoro (that is, the outside west wall of the enclosed choir) has carvings of Saints Peter and Paul, which are neglected by most visitors in favour of the Papamoscas, the moustachioed figure who chants the time from the nearby sixteenth-century clock.

The whole cathedral is garlanded with a gallery with bays. Then that symmetry is abandoned and the side chapels seem to have been pleasingly added at random. To begin exploring them at the north-west corner of the cathedral is to open with a burst of churrigueresque magic: the mid eighteenth-century vault and cupola of the Capilla de Santa Tecla sets off perfectly the cool skills of the sculptor who carved its twelfth-century romanesque font. The next chapel along, the Capilla Santa Ana, was built three centuries earlier by Simón de Colonia, the son of Juan de Colonia. Bishop Luis Osorio de Acuña, who died in 1495, lies here in a tomb by Diego de Siloé. Another Flamboyant gothic tomb of the same date shelters the body of Archdeacon Díaz. But the greatest delight of this chapel is its late gothic reredos depicting a Tree of Jesse, gilded against a blue background, the work of Gil de Siloé and Diego de la Cruz.

One of the glories of Burgos cathedral now comes into view in the north transept. The golden, balustraded staircase, which doubles back on to itself as it rises to the thirteenth-century Puerta de la Coronería, was created by Diego de Siloé in 1519 at the behest of Bishop Fonseca, whose coat of arms decorates it. Beyond this transept appear successively the thirteenth-century chapel of San Nicolás, which houses the tomb of Bishop Juan de Villahoz who died in 1275, the Capilla de la Natividad, with a late sixteenth-century reredos by Martín de la Haya, and the fourteenth-century Capilla de la Asunción, with another gothic tomb. Fourteenth-century gothic tombs also fill the next chapel, the Capilla de San Gregorio.

We have now reached another gem of Burgos cathedral, the Capilla del Condestable, which was built in the 1480s in a flamboyant plateresque style by Simón de Colonia for Pedro Hernández de Velasco, Constable of Castile. Cristóbal Andino made its superb screen and Diego de Siloé was responsible for its reredos, a magnificent work devoted to the Presentation of Jesus in the Jerusalem Temple. The huge coats of arms flanking it are probably by Gil de Siloé. In 1492 the chapel's founder died. Pedro Hernández de Velasco lies in a tomb on which is his effigy, sculpted in white Carrara marble, in all probability by Felipe Vigarni, and beside him is his wife, Doña Mencia de Mendoza, who died two years after him. The massive coats of arms on the walls flanking the altar-piece belong to the Mendozas and the Velascos. Adjoining the Capilla del Condestable is the Capilla de Santiago, built in the decade beginning in 1524 by Juan de Vallejo. Its screen, which is hard to make out in the gloom of this part of the cathedral, carries a wild depiction of Santiago Matamoros.

On leaving this chapel, walk to the west end of the cathedral, and enter the late thirteenth-century gothic cloisters by way of the fourteenth-century Puerta del Claustro, whose doors are carved with renaissance scenes of Jesus entering Jerusalem and visiting Hades. The limestone portal is sculpted with depictions of the Annunciation, King David, the Prophet Isaiah and Jesus's Baptism. Statues which have found no place in the cathedral are stored in this cloister and are nonetheless well worth a glance, especially those of King Ferdinando the Saint and his wife Beatriz. Fine chapels open off the cloister, in particular the Capilla de Santa Catalina, whose capitals are carved with scenes from a hunt. And in the Capilla del Corpus Cristi hangs a venerable eleventh-century chest. It belonged to El Cid. Short of cash to finance his wars, he filled it with iron and sand and persuaded the Jews of Burgos that the contents were his entire treasure, at which

Burgos: a detail of the fountain in Plaza Santa Maria.

they readily financed his adventures. Beyond this chapel is the chapter-house, with a lovely coffered and painted artesonado ceiling.

Re-enter the cathedral at the west end and you will find three more exquisite chapels. The Capilla de la Visitación was created by Juan de Colonia, who sculpted the recumbent figure of his patron and promoter, Bishop Alonso de Cartagena. In the early sixteenth-century Capilla de la Presentación, whose grille was wrought by Cristóbal Andino, is an altar painting of the Madonna by Sebastiano del Piombo, along with four sixteenth-century tombs. Finally, the Capilla del Santísimo Cristo is, for the faithful, the greatest of all. Believers crowd to kneel humbly before a late sixteenth-century Christ, evidently taken from a Deposition, furnished with human hair and eyebrows and traditionally attributed to St Nicodemus, who offered the dead Jesus a grave.

Another celebrated episode associated with the legendary El Cid occurred in the gothic church of Santa

55

Agueda, to the west of the cathedral. Here Rodrigo Díaz forced King Alfonso VI to swear that he had no part in the murder of his brother Sancho. Alfonso was reluctant to swear, until a knight shouted that no king had ever been found guilty of perjury, just as no pope had ever been excommunicated. At this the king took the oath three times, once by the cross at the entrance to the church, a second time beside the bolt of the door, and finally at the high altar.

Make your way east from the cathedral by way of Plaza de José Antonio to the Casa del Cordón. Built towards the end of the fifteenth century for Constable Hernández de Velasco, its name derives from the girdle of St Francis of Assisi over the main doorway linking the armoury with the domestic quarters. Although the walls of the house are rustic in style, the stones of the portal are mighty, and the emblem of a shining sun and the escutcheons of the Mendoza family and of Pedro Hernández de Velasco sculpted on the pediment are expansive. The house, with its lovely patio, has witnessed some historic moments: Christopher Columbus, returned from his second expedition, was received here by Ferdinand and Isabella; and Felipe the Beautiful died here, leaving the throne of Spain to Emperor Charles V. A wild, bearded and mounted El Cid dominates the plaza to the south of here.

From here you should cross the river and drive east for 3 kilometres along Avenida Conde Vallellano, which is flanked by plantations of poplars and elms, to the charterhouse known as the Cartuja de Miraflores. It stands where Enrique III had built a palace and laid out a park towards the end of the fourteenth century. The Arco de la Vieja, over whose doorway are the initials J C R R R ('Jesus Cristus Redemptor Rex Regum'), still stands at the entrance to the park. The Carthusians settled here in 1441. Within ten years their monastery had burned to the ground, and we owe the present building to Juan and Simón de Colonia. They built for the monks a Flamboyant gothic church whose nave was constructed so as to separate the lay brothers from the ordained brothers, and both of them from the faithful who had made no Carthusian profession. Martín Sánchez sculpted gothic stalls for the ordained

monks in 1488, and in 1558 the lay brethren were provided with magnificent renaissance stalls, the work of Simón de Bueras.

Juan II, father of Isabella the Catholic and royal patron of this monastery, lies in a late fifteenth-century tomb by Gil de Siloé in front of the high altar; beside him is his second wife, Isabella of Portugal. In the 1490s the same sculptor carved the wooden reredos of the Life of Christ for the Capilla Mayor. Juan and Isabella put in an appearance here too, along with Jesus, the Virgin Mary, St John the Evangelist and the pelican in its piety, eating into its own flesh to feed its little ones. Look out for the tomb of the infant brother of Isabella of Castile. The prince died in 1470, aged eleven, and is represented here in a riotously elaborate niche, kneeling before his sarcophagus, with a cherub swinging in a tree behind him. The whole ensemble is again the work of Gil de Siloé. Here too is a beautiful baroque statue of St James the Great, gilded and painted. With swirling beard, a cockle shell on his hat and holding a scrip, he has evidently come far, for his toes peep through his worn-out boots.

This monastery has seen hard times, especially as a result of the secularization which forced the monks to leave in 1835. Théophile Gautier, visiting Burgos shortly afterwards, feared that the splendid buildings would fall into ruin. 'Cut one another's throats in the name of the ideal which you imagine yourselves to possess, and manure the stricken, war-ravaged fields with corpses, but the stone, marble and bronze shaped by the hand of genius are sacred', he urged. 'In two thousand years your civil discords will have been forgotten, and future generations will learn that you were a great nation only from marvellous fragments unearthed by archaeology.' Fortunately, the religious have returned, and the Cartuja de Miraflores is once more in mint condition.

Six kilometres further east, along a pine-shaded road, stands the Benedictine monastery of San Pedro

The arched gateway built at Burgos in honour of the Virgin Mary and the Holy Roman Emperor Charles V.

The entrance to the convent of Las Huelgas on the outskirts of Burgos.

de Cardeña. Founded in the eleventh century, it is celebrated as the spot to which El Cid confided his wife and children when he was banned from Castile, and as we have seen he wished to be buried here. His favourite horse, Babieca, was buried nearby. Today the monastic buildings mostly date from the eighteenth century.

Drive back across the river over the Puente de Santa María, the five-arched bridge fronting the arrogant gateway which Emperor Charles V in 1536 decreed should celebrate the glories of the Blessed Virgin Mary, but in the end served only to glamorize the emperor himself. The citizens of Burgos were obliged to build it in penitence for their part in the revolt of the *comuneros*. A statue of the Blessed Virgin does occupy the topmost niche, but pride of place is given to the Holy Roman Emperor, who is accompanied by two judges, Nuño Rasura and Lain Calvo, two counts, Diego Porcelos and Fernán González, and El Cid.

From here drive west along Avenida del Generalísimo Franco, recross the river and continue west to visit the Real Monasterío de las Huelgas and the Hospital del Rey. *Huelgas* means leisure times, and King Alfonso VIII and his wife Eleanor of England founded the nunnery in 1175 on the site of a royal pleasure palace. Over the gateway sits the placid figure of the apostle St James the Great, and on the plateresque portal of the hospital he is sculpted slaying Moors, a couple of their severed heads beneath the hooves of his charger.

A Cistercian foundation, the convent of Las Huelgas was designated only for the daughters of the noble and royal houses of Spain. The Cistercians' commitment to a life of extreme austerity is attested by the architecture of this monastery, whose church, dating from 1180 to 1215, and other monastic quarters, built between 1215 and 1230, are typically severe in style. Nonetheless, the foundation inevitably inherited sumptuous treasures: sixteenth-century Beauvais tapestries, mannerist sculptures of the school of Juan de Juni, a sixteenth-century reredos from the workshop of Diego de Siloé, Flemish triptychs and thirteenth-century stained-glass windows. The founders lie in twin tombs in the chapel. Spanish christendom's eternal preoccupation is revealed by a banner taken in battle from the Moors in 1212. The twelfth-century romanesque cloisters have twin columns and give on to a polylobe-arched *mudéjar* chapel. And in the chapel of Santiago is kept a quaint statue of St James with moveable arms, used in the past to confer knighthoods on members of his order.

A couple of kilometres further on is the Hospital del Rey, set up as a pilgrims' hospital in the twelfth century and rebuilt in the sixteenth; its plateresque doorway dates from 1526.

The plethora of stunningly sited villages and towns around Burgos is overwhelming. To pick one at random from the country to the north, Frías has white houses with balconies, some of which rest on sturdy,

The Laguna Negra de Neila, south-east of Burgos.

round, stone arcading, others on apparently crumbling wooden pillars which hardly seem capable of supporting the cross-beams, let alone the balcony above. The bridge over the River Ebro supports not only a medieval defensive tower but also all manner of vegetation. A time-weathered medieval *castillo* still pretends to protect the town.

From the city of Burgos, take the N234 to the south-east towards Soria and turn left to Quintanilla de las Viñas. Just outside the village is a Visigothic church dating from the seventh century, for which its builders cannibalized Roman columns. For another exquisite town of arcaded streets and half-timbered houses, turn right from the N234 to the ancient town of Covarrubias. Here beside the river, amidst fragmentary walls and an early sixteenth-century gateway, rise the ruins of a tenth-century palace and the tower of Doña Urraca. Fernán González, the first count of Castile, and his wife lie in tombs inside the fifteenth-century collegiate church. In the first chapel on the left is a sixteenth-century triptych carved by Diego de Siloé, depicting the adoration of the Magi, which was painted by Diego de la Cruz. The town hall of Covarrubias dates from the sixteenth century and has plateresque windows designed by Juan de Vallejo. As one might imagine, the renaissance architect Alonso de Covarrubias, who has already provided us with much pleasure, was born here.

Further south-east is one of the most evocative Benedictine monasteries in Spain. Although the church was rebuilt by Ventura Rodríguez in the eighteenth century, the cloisters of Santo Domingo de Silos date from the eleventh century; the green lawns, roses and trees of the cloister garden are sheltered by a double row of arches supporting an upper gallery. Birds intricately intertwine their necks on some of the capitals, while on others are carved the stylized plants beloved of romanesque sculptors. The eleventh-century saint who rebuilt this monastery after the

In the romanesque cloister of Santo Domingo de Silos: Jesus on the road to Emmaus.

Moors had sacked it lies in a fourteenth-century sarcophagus in these cloisters. Around 100,000 volumes, including incunables and codices, fill the monastery library; and preserved intact is the eighteenth-century dispensary, with blue-glazed pots and jars still on their original shelves.

Wind westwards from here along the valley of the Río Arlanza to Lerma, whose ducal palace, designed by Francisco de Mora in 1617, stands on the site of an earlier fortress, and whose collegiate church dates from the early seventeenth century. All that remains of Lerma's twelfth-century walls is a romanesque gateway. The road runs on westwards from here to join the E82, which will take you south-west to Palencia.

Though the cathedral of Palencia was begun in 1321, the building which rises just east of the Río Carrión today, with its tall, square belfry, is an unfinished masterpiece of late fifteenth-century Spanish architecture. One feels the lack of a respectably ornate façade,

At Frías this medieval bridge spanning the Ebro was one of the traditional gateways into Old Castile.

but the decorated doorways, above all the complex south portal in the paved Plaza de la Immacola Concepción, make up for it. Known as the Puerto del Obispo, it was designed by Diego Hurtado de Mendoza in the late fifteenth century. Signs of the zodiac, sculpted gothic arches and a statue of the Madonna are surmounted by a statue of St Antonin of Pamiers, patron of the cathedral and the city and known to the Spanish as Antolín.

Annually Palencia celebrates his feast with a fair lasting from 28 September to 3 October. Martyred at Palencia, he was buried on the site now occupied by the cathedral. Sancho the Great is said to have discovered here not the saint's bones but a statuette depicting the martyr. (At any rate, a plateresque flight of steps just in front of the trascoro invites you to descend to the Visigothic crypt where this momentous discovery took place.)

But we are not yet inside the cathedral. In addition to the statue of St Antolín, the saints, kings and prophets in the arches of the Puerta del Obispo are animated enough; but I like best the little creatures who swarm half-hidden among the foliage. I suggest now that you climb the tower to orientate yourself on this part of Castile, with the hills of Ostero and San Juan in the distance and to the west, stretching even further away, the Tierra de Campos.

The cathedral's ample interior, progressively widened from the fourteenth to the sixteenth century, has clustered columns from which rises the delicate vaulting of its nave and aisles. Elaborate though the vaults may be, they pale beside the plateresque wonders of this cathedral: the retable of the high altar in the Capilla Mayor, which dates from 1530; the chapel of the Blessed Sacrament; and the doorway by Alonso Berruguete which leads to the cloisters.

Of these the retable of the Capilla Mayor is unquestionably the greatest treasure of Palencia cathedral. Cristóbal Andino made the wrought-iron grille which

Near the hermitage of San Pedro de Arlanza, east of Covarrubias.

A statue of the Virgin Mary outside the cathedral of Palencia.

screens the chapel in 1572. The high altar was designed by the plateresque master Pedro de Guadalupe in 1504, and the following year Philip of Burgundy sculpted its statues. Neither artist supposed he was working on the central altar of the cathedral, for their work was originally intended for the sacristy. Before the altarpiece reached its present exalted position, Juan de Flandes spent a decade, from 1510, working on its paintings, Juan de Valmaseda carved its Calvary in 1519 and five years later Gonzalo de la Maza and Alonso de Solórzano added their own sculptures.

In the nave the triforium arcading matches the windows of the clerestory in its exquisite ornamentation. As if there were little more anyone could do to enhance such masterly architecture, later builders turned their attention to the choir, whose stalls date from the mid seventeenth century. Gaspar Rodríguez made the plateresque wrought-iron choir screen in 1555. The hand of Gil de Siloé in the trascoro ensures

63

that sixteenth-century gothic triumphs at least in this part of the cathedral. Higínio Balmaseda contributed a pulpit so floridly carved that preachers must have been in grave danger of haranguing the faithful in equally overwrought prose. The altar-piece, just as elaborate, is by Juan de Holanda, who came from Haarlem, and its eight panels depict the Virgin Mary and St John flanked by scenes from the life of Jesus. Immodestly, Bishop Fonseca, donor of the altar-piece, ordered the artist to portray him beside the Madonna.

Palencia cathedral is a church of great altar-pieces. That behind the high altar, to take just one, is a huge classical affair by Felipe Vigarni. Jesus, uniformly dressed in black – save when naked for burial and in the resurrection scene, in which he wears a crimson cloak – is the subject of the lower panels. Above these scenes the altar-piece is taken over by his saints and disciples and above all the Blessed Virgin Mary. In the upper panels the four major scenes depict her receiving the Angel Gabriel, calling on her similarly pregnant cousin Elizabeth, adoring her infant son, and proudly presenting him to the Magi.

Splendid tombs add lustre to the building. Against the outer walls of the Capilla Mayor are the sixteenth-century sepulchres of three abbots: Diego de Guevára (which dates from 1509), Rodrigo Enríquez and Francisco Nuñes. Another superb tomb is that of Dean Husillos. His recumbent statue is the only serene element in a busily gothic decor. Did those whose dust crumbles here expect us to enjoy so much their last earthly resting places? Whether they did or not, they are certainly a source of pleasure, and I particularly liked two earlier tombs, those of Doña Urraca de Navarra, sculpted in the twelfth century, and of Doña Inés de Osorio, which dates from 1492.

As for painters, Francisco Zurbarán contributed to Palencia cathedral one of those monumental portraits of meditating saints which made him famous in the 1630s, this one, in the Capilla de Santa Lucía, depicting St Catherine at prayer. To admire Juan de Villoldo's paintings of the Transfiguration and the Purification you must make your way to the sacristy of the Capilla de San Gregorio.

The finest part of the monastic buildings connected with Palencia cathedral comprises the rooms of its chapter-house, whose four superb Flemish tapestries depict the Adoration of the Magi, the Raising of Lazarus and the Seven Deadly Sins. These buildings house the cathedral museum and display yet more tapestries, all from the Low Countries, all priceless. Among the other treasures do not miss a diptych by Pedro Berruguete.

Clearly, while amassing such treasures, the clergy of Palencia Cathedral did not neglect the seven cardinal virtues, and adjoining their house of God is a twelfth-century hospice dedicated to St Barnabas and St Antolín. Rebuilt in the fifteenth century, it was re-endowed by Doña Maria de Mendoza in 1580, when its grim façade was humanized by a renaissance doorway. Though much eroded, the comical beasts on this portal still grin down on to the pollarded plane trees of the Plaza de Cervantes.

Calle General Mola runs along the west end of the cathedral. If you follow it to the south you reach the episcopal palace, which now serves as a museum of sacred art. To the north, Calle General Mola leads to the romanesque-gothic church of San Miguel, whose crenellated belfry served also as a defensive tower, which the parishioners contrived to make less menacing by piercing the walls with slender gothic windows. Legend has it that El Cid was married in this church, some say in front of its thirteenth-century Crucifix, though this seems unlikely since he died in 1099.

The earthquake which destroyed Lisbon in 1755 left the tall and elegant nave of this church badly askew. A chapel on the left has fine roof bosses, and over the renaissance sepulchre of Pablo González Jesus's own entombment is depicted; but the most exquisite work of art in San Miguel is a fourteenth-century fresco in the south aisle. Here St Michael slays the dragon and St Francis of Assisi receives the stigmata, while beneath

---

An arcaded street totters crazily at Ampúdia, which is situated 24 kilometres south-west of Palencia at the heart of the Tierra de Campos.

them are St John the Baptist, the Lamb of God, and St Onofret naked in the desert.

Walk back along the *calle* and turn first right to find the church of Nuestra Señora de la Calle, with its harmonious seventeenth-century façade. The church faces Calle General Franco, which you should follow, turning left along the pedestrianized Calle Mayor, with its arcades, overhanging balconies and elegant shop fronts, to reach Palencia's arcaded Plaza Mayor, with the ubiquitous pollarded planes and a classical town hall. That the Romans inhabited this neighbourhood is attested by the Roman tombstones on display here in the Ayuntamiento's Archaeological Museum (along with some fine romanesque and gothic sculptures).

In rapid succession this little cathedral city reveals three of its remaining four treasures, interspersed with other delights. Just across the Plaza Mayor is the fourteenth-century gothic church of San Francisco, with a massive atrium or colonnaded porch. Above it are four open belfries containing three bells each, and on top of the two smaller belfries perch statues of Franciscan monks. Below them is a delicate thirteenth-century rose window. San Francisco abuts on to the chapel of La Soledad, which enshrines a fourteenth-century statue of the Blessed Virgin Mary.

Walk from the other side of the Plaza Mayor, past the Diputación (County Hall), which resembles a giant ice-cream cake, and turn left into Calle Burgos, which will take you successively to the churches of Santa Clara and San Lázaro. The most grisly sight inside the late fourteenth-century gothic Santa Clara is a recumbent figure, claimed by believers to be Jesus but declared by sceptics to be a mummy washed up by the Atlantic Ocean. Gazing on this gruesome object I am much inclined to take the side of the sceptics. In a baroque chapel, St Francis (whose sister founded the order of nuns, members of which are usually praying behind the grille of the choir at the west end of the church) is depicted ecstatically receiving the stigmata.

Drum-shaped dovecotes dotting the landscape at Amusco on the edge of the Tierra de Campos.

On the other side of Calle Burgos rises the delicate classical façade of the Teatro Principal. San Lázaro, with a simple square belfry, is worth a visit simply for its six panels by Juan de Flandes depicting scenes from the life of Jesus. Another curious painting in this church is a copy of an Andrea del Sarto Madonna.

The final architectural delight of Palencia, the fifteenth-century church of San Pablo, stands in the northern quarter of the city. Built for the Dominicans in 1217 and rebuilt in the gothic style in the fifteenth century, its renaissance façade exactly parallels in its austerity the rigour of their rule of life. Inside, however, austerity gives way to elegance, with gothic vaulting spanning the nave and aisles, while the choir stalls and the polychrome plateresque reredos of the Capilla Mayor both derive from the late sixteenth century. A gothic altar in the north transept stands beneath a sculpted Pietà, and the tombs of the marquises of Poza display the sumptuous arrogance of Alonso Berruguete and Pompeo Leoni – matched by Francisco Giralte's 1557 tomb of the Rojas family.

Frómista lies almost due north of Palencia by way of such treats as Fuentes de Valdepero, with its sixteenth-century *castillo*, and Monzón de Campos, whose medieval fortress is now a hotel. The fertile landscape is occasionally enlivened by conical shepherds' huts and drum-shaped dovecotes. A few kilometres further on from Monzón de Campos, a massive church dominates the village of Amusco, one of its doorways decorated with signs of the zodiac, the other guarded by statues of saints Peter and Paul. And after another 5 kilometres the eight round towers of the ruined castle of Piña de Campos come into view.

At Frómista itself awaits the exquisite church of San Martín, a couple of round romanesque towers on either side of its west façade and an octagonal lantern rising over the triple apse, with its chequerboard decoration. Doña Elvira, widow of Sancho the Great of Navarre, built the church in 1066 (as well as a now disappeared monastery) for Benedictine monks. San Martín is so fine that one could easily neglect the other churches of Frómista, particularly Santa María del Castillo, a late gothic church with a sixteenth-century reredos painted by Juan de Flandes, and San Pedro, again gothic but with a renaissance doorway and reredos, as well as eighteenth-century paintings by Anton Raphaël Mengs. Pause too in the Plaza Mayor. The figure balancing on a coracle in a little pool is St Telmo, patron of sailors, who was born at Frómista in 1190.

We have now joined a major pilgrimage route to Santiago de Compostela, though Población de Campos, the first village west of Frómista, has a church dedicated not to St James but to San Miguel. Santiago makes his mark in a chapel of the thirteenth-century church of Santa María la Blanca at the tumbledown village of Villalcázar de Sirga, and a yet more triumphant appearance at Carrión de los Condes, where in a narrow twisting street the church dedicated to the saint has a magnificent romanesque portal.

From here the pilgrimage route to Santiago de Compostela takes us through well cultivated countryside to Sahagún. Sahagún was once an exceedingly rich town, partly because of its situation on two rivers and partly because for centuries Jews, French, Moors and Christians lived here in harmony, though with their own separate quarters. Of its sometime nine medieval churches, four survive, as well as the Franciscan church of La Pellegrina just outside the town.

All the churches are built to the same plan, with blind arcades and a massive square belfry rising from the choir. The oldest is San Tirso, built in the twelfth century and standing today beside the ruins of a twelfth-century Benedictine monastery. Fleeing from the Arabs in the tenth century, monks from Córdoba eventually established their headquarters at Sahagún. The order is still represented here by a group of Benedictine nuns who live in a convent nearby.

Built almost entirely of brick, whose different colours delicately pattern the walls, San Tirso is a fine example of the romanesque-*mudéjar* style. It is not however, the finest church in the town. A quiet street curves down from the top of Sahagún to San Lorenzo, a thirteenth-century romanesque masterpiece whose blind arcades follow *mudéjar* curves and whose apse is embellished with a horseshoe arch. On the south side of the church is a romanesque colonnade.

From Sahagún sparsely wooded, gentle rolling countryside flanks the 13 kilometres to Gordaliza del Pino. Beyond this village, passing through a landscape with quaint troglodytic dwellings, you meet the N601 and turn right for León. Just beyond Santa Cristina de Madrigal turn left and continue for 17 kilometres to Valencia de Don Juan, where you will see the moated fourteenth-century fortress which once belonged to the counts of Oñate. Though ruined, it retains the round bastions which support its crenellated walls, and its massive keep, with six attached round towers, still rises majestically from the rocks above the left bank of the Río Esla. The churches in Valencia de Don Juan are worth seeing for their fine reredoses, that in San Augustín attributed to the pupils of Juan de Juni, that in San Pedro sculpted in the 1540s by Guillermo Doncel. The town derives its name from Don Juan of Portugal, Duke of Valencia in the fourteenth century.

León lies due north. On the way, veer right after 20 kilometres and drive along the Esla valley to rejoin the N601 at the fortified village of Mansilla de las Mulas. Its medieval defensive walls are the finest in the province, though the eastern gateway of the village remains barely intact. The fourteenth-century church of San Martín and an early sixteenth-century Augustinian convent have both been put to secular uses. The prettiest part of the town today is its arcaded Plaza Mayor.

Scarcely a kilometre beyond Mansilla de las Mulas, follow the signpost on the right-hand side of the road to the romanesque monastery of San Miguel de Escalada. It was founded in 913 by monks from Córdoba who wished to escape the dominance of the Moors. Eleven delicate cusped arches support an outside gallery, the oldest Mozarabic gallery of this kind in Spain. Steps lead down into the adjoining church, which was finished in the mid twelfth century. Its three aisles are divided by horseshoe arches rising from marble pillars with stylized capitals.

The romanesque church of San Tirso at Sahagún stands in front of the ruined monastery of San Benito.

The road from Mansilla de las Mulas runs on towards León through an increasingly inhospitable landscape. Then the wooded valley of the Río Bernesga opens its arms with a gentle welcome to the provincial capital. This is today an industrial city, but the moment you reach the arcaded Plaza Santa Ana you find yourself on the outskirts of a district of narrow, picturesque medieval streets. The little romanesque church of Santa Ana once belonged to the Knights of St John of Jerusalem and is still marked by their Maltese cross.

You have to park here and walk along Calle Barahona, through the city walls to the narrower, irregular and cobbled Calle de Puerta Moneda. Medieval streets surround the twelfth-century church of Santa María del Camiño, one of the stops on the pilgrimage route to Santiago da Compostela (*camino* or *camiño* is Spanish for 'road'). Its round apse juts into the plaza of the same name, which is shaded by a couple of massive elm trees and cooled by a neo-classical fountain of 1789. The medieval and renaissance houses have balconies rising from pillars and overhanging the square.

Calle de Herreros continues to the Convento de la Concepcíon, which stands in a triangular plaza, its projecting balcony decorated with a painted frieze, its entrance a little renaissance treat. Beyond it the medieval Calle de la Rúa leads to Plazuela San Marcelo, with its Doric and Ionic Ayuntamiento, or city hall, built by Juan del Rivero in 1585, and the church of San Marcelo, dedicated to one of the patron saints of León, a second-century Roman legionary who was martyred because he refused to renounce Christianity.

His church, rebuilt in the sixteenth century by Baltasár Gutiérrez and Juan del Rivero, has a sumptuous reredos sculpted by Gregorio Fernández, in the middle of which the patron saint stands resolute. By contrast, in Fernández's crucifixion scene in the same church, Jesus half-closes his eyes in despair. Nearby is a group of buildings remarkable for being decorated all over with the cockle shells of St James of Compostela. Their extravagance pales, however, beside the late nineteenth-century Casa de los Botines. This bizarre building was designed as a private home by the Catalan art nouveau architect Antonio Gaudí. Its serpentine arches and sinuous ironwork are recognizably his own, but one can readily perceive the influence of Gaudí's *mudéjar* predecessors. Nearby stands the Palacio de los Guzmanes, which was built in 1560 for a Bishop of Calahorra, Quiñones and Guzman by Rodrigo Gil de Hontañón. The two-storey patio is plateresque.

From this palace Calle del Generalísimo Franco runs eastwards to the cathedral of Santa María de la Regla – built on the site of the old Roman baths, for León was once a fortified Roman camp and derives its name from the seventh Roman legion which was stationed here. León is in the far north of Castile, but this fact alone does not account for the remarkable French influence on this cathedral, whose ground plan (with three naves and three transepts) is modelled in part on the cathedral at Reims, while the west façade resembles that of Amiens. (French architectural styles were also brought here by medieval pilgrims on the way to Santiago de Compostela.) Of the three west portals, the left-hand one carries scenes from the early years of the Infant Jesus, beginning with the Annunciation, continuing with the Nativity and ending with the Adoration of the Magi, the Flight into Egypt and the Massacre of the Innocents. Mary is the theme of the right-hand portal, which depicts her falling asleep and her heavenly coronation. A white stone statue of the Virgin Mary, Nuestra Señora la Blanca, stands between the doors of the central portal. In its tympanum is a Last Judgment, in which the just are entertained with sacred music while the damned are cooked and then eaten by devils.

Above a huge rose window is a gable sculpted with a relief of the Annunciation and a statue of Jesus. A pair of towers of unequal height flank the façade, the northern one the earlier, the southern one dubbed the Torre de Reloj. Built in the fifteenth century, its openwork spire rises to five storeys, the cornice of the first one inscribed MARIA – JESVS XPS – DEVS HOMO

The damned receive their just reward in this lively carving on the west portal of León cathedral.

Some of the finest stained glass on León cathedral gleams from this rose window in the north transept.

('Mary, Jesus Christ, God made man') and AVE MARIA – GRATIA PLENA – DOMINVS TECUM ('Hail Mary, full of grace, the Lord is with thee'). Elegant flying buttresses support the southern side of the building.

León cathedral was built fast and is thus remarkably unified. Bishop Manrique de Lara laid the foundation stone in 1199, after which symbolic act work virtually ceased for half a century. Then King Sancho IV took up the task in the 1290s, and through his patronage the building was finished and consecrated in 1303. Capped by ogival vaulting, it stretches for 90 metres from west to east, while its nave rises at the centre to 39 metres, almost exactly matching the total width of the building. Nearly 3000 square metres of stained glass, which fill 57 lights and three enormous rose windows, illuminate the interior, much of it dating from the thirteenth and fourteenth centuries.

The cathedral furnishings are sumptuous. The main reredos, by Nicolás Francés, has three panels devoted to the life of St Froilán and a fourth depicting the Presentation of Mary in the Temple of Jerusalem; above all four is a scene showing bullocks dragging the coffin of St James the Great to Galicia. In the choir are two magnificent thrones, one for the bishop, the other for the sovereign, who was designated an honorary canon of this cathedral. Flemish craftsmen carved out of black walnut the 76 mid fifteenth-century stalls. The richness of this choir is matched by the gilded alabaster trascoro. The angel humbly kneels before the Virgin Mary in the relief of the Annunciation carved here by Estéban Jordán in 1576.

Through a richly decorated doorway on the north side of the apse you enter the plateresque Capilla de Santiago, which was built by Juan de Badajoz in the mid sixteenth century. Lit by glowing stained glass, its vaulted ceiling springs from a frieze of acanthus leaves, angels, men and mythical beasts. On the capitals of the pillars Samson wrestles with a lion, a dim-witted monk attempts to read (accompanied by the inscription *legere non intelligere*, 'to read without understanding') and a giant writhes in the coils of a serpent. On the altar the Madonna supports the massive corpse of her dead son, and in a niche behind her sits St James the Great.

West of the cathedral rises the royal collegiate church of San Isidoro, with its sturdy romanesque belfry known as the Torre del Gallo because of the cock on its weather vane. One of the numerous patron saints of Spain, St Isidore had originally been buried in Toledo cathedral, but when the Moors ruled that part of Spain King Ferdinando I of Castile and León managed to persuade them to sell him Isidore's relics. Before then, all that stood on this spot was a church dedicated to St John the Baptist. At the end of the tenth century Al Mansour had demolished it, but under the patronage of King Alfonso V it had been rebuilt. Ferdinand I now decided to transform it into a church worthy of the bones he had just acquired.

This royal basilica has two elaborately carved romanesque entrances. The first one, the Puerta del Cordero (Door of the Lamb of God) is sculpted with a frieze of the signs of the zodiac and, in the tympanum, a depiction of Abraham sacrificing Isaac; in the gable

The plateresque façade which Juan de Badajoz designed for the hospice of San Marcos, León.

This detail of the hospice façade depicts the emblem of the Knights of Santiago.

above is a massive, eighteenth-century statue of St Isidore on horseback. He also appears, less arrogantly, in a romanesque statue to the left of the doorway, added in the eighteenth century. The tympanum of the right-hand portal, the Puerta del Perdón (Door of Forgiveness), is carved with a Deposition in which a man with huge pincers pulls a nail out of the left hand of the dead Saviour.

Inside the basilica are romanesque pillars with exquisite carved capitals. The font is square, roman-esque and sculpted. Enrique de Arfe made the basilica's chased processional cross. Multi-lobed *mudéjar* arches support the vaulting of the transepts. St Isidore lies in a reliquary on the high altar of the Capilla Mayor, which is protected by an elaborate screen and backed by a gothic reredos in which the Holy Sacrament is permanently exposed.

Ferdinand I brought Isidore's bones to León to lend sanctity to his own less than saintly remains, for he wished to set up here a royal pantheon. The *Pantéon de los Reyes de León*, with its delicate Mozarabic palms and pineapples, was built between 1054 and 1066. Eleven kings, twelve queens and twenty-one other members of the León royal house lie here. To the twentieth-century visitor this royal dust is boring compared with the frescoes which were painted inside the pantheon around 1160. A Byzantine Christ Pantocrator in a mandorla blesses us, surrounded by the symbols of Matthew, Mark, Luke and John. The Saviour holds open a book inscribed in Latin, 'I am the light of the world'. In blue, ochre and red, life on earth is represented by paintings of the labours of each month (with the grapes being harvested in September and pigs snuffling for truffles in October). While in one scene angels proclaim the birth of Jesus, in another stags indulge in ritual combat.

Calle de Rey Nueva and Calle Suena de Quiñones lead to the outrageously splendid hospice of San

Marcos, which stands beside the Río Bernesga. Here, in the mid twelfth century, Queen Doña Sancha set up a church and a tiny pilgrims' hospice. By the end of the century it had been taken into the care of the recently founded order of the Knights of Santiago, whose duties involved defending all those journeying to the shrine of St James in Galicia, caring for the ones who fell ill and burying any who should die on their way to or from Santiago de Compostela. Meeting at Valladolid in 1513, the knights agreed that the hospice, its church and its cloister should be completely rebuilt, and further decided that the work should be entrusted to the plateresque master Juan de Badajoz.

For the hospice itself Juan de Badajoz designed a façade which stretches for some 100 metres, its horizontal lines broken by slender columned windows topped with pilasters. Beneath a multi-lobed *mudéjar* arch over the central doorway is the figure of Santiago Matamoros, the Moors falling beneath his sword and the hooves of his charger. On either side extends a row of portrait medallions, depicting heroes and heroines of the Old and New Testaments, of the pagan ages and the Christian era – all of them the work of Juan de Badajoz and his colleague Juan de Horozco. Some of their juxtapositions are judicious. They took care to flatter the Holy Roman Emperor Charles V by placing him between Augustus Caesar and Trajan.

Beside the hospice stands a powerfully built chapel, its west front ornamented with countless cockle shells. Inside, under a cusped gothic ceiling, more cockle shells stud an enormous gallery. Juan de Juni and his colleagues carved the elaborate two-tier stalls for the canons.

A bridge has spanned the Río Bernesga at this point since Roman times, though the existing bridge is medieval. Beyond it stretches the harsh countryside of the *Maragatos*, the ancient muleteers whose descendants still live in this part of Castile. Another medieval bridge crosses the Río Orbigo, where an old pilgrims'

An unmistakable example of the genius of Antonio Gaudí: the episcopal palace at Astorga.

hospice today stands in ruins. Then the landscape starts to undulate, with fruit trees and vines softening its aspect, until suddenly across a valley appears the cathedral of Astorga.

From its sixteenth-century plateresque façade (dominated by a statue of St James the Great and attributed to Rodrigo Gil de Hontañón) a baroque doorway opens into a richly decorated cathedral whose late gothic vaults are painted and gilded. The reredos and walnut stalls date from the sixteenth century, the former sculpted by Gaspar Becerra who had studied in the workshops of Roman masters. Astorga also has a baroque Ayuntamiento and a late nineteenth-century episcopal palace by Antonio Gaudí at his most playful. Yet as a historian of Spanish cathedrals, John Harvey, has observed, Astorga seems melancholy and lost, 'a strange and lonely city, facing westwards towards the heaped-up ranges of mountains which divide Spain from Galicia'.

Vineyards flourish in the countryside of El Bierzo south of Ponferrada.

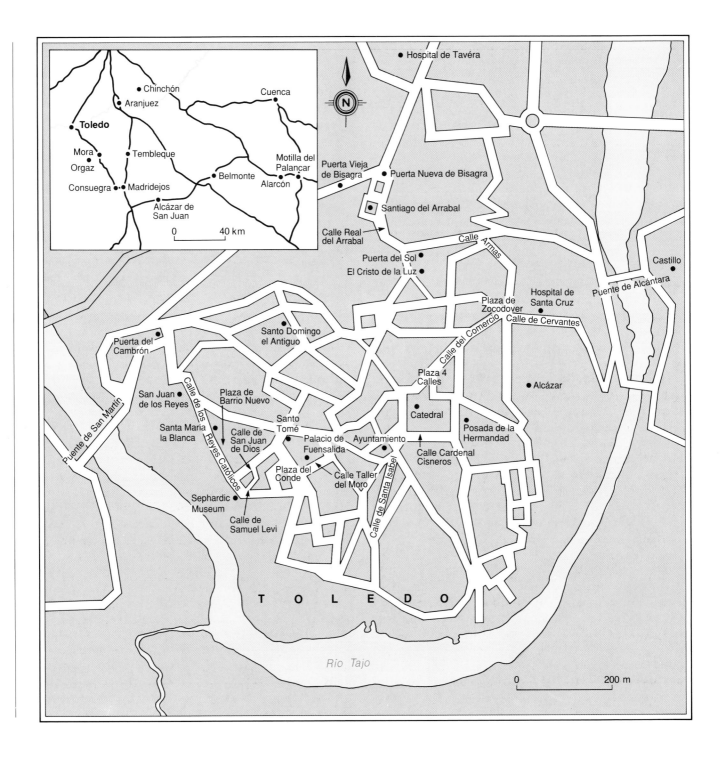

Hospital de Tavéra

Puerta Vieja de Bisagra
Puerta Nueva de Bisagra
Santiago del Arrabal
Calle Real del Arrabal
Calle Armas
Puerta del Sol
El Cristo de la Luz
Castillo
Puente de Alcántara
Plaza de Zocodover
Hospital de Santa Cruz
Calle de Cervantes

Puerta del Cambrón
Santo Domingo el Antiguo
Calle del Comercio
Plaza 4 Calles
Alcázar

San Juan de los Reyes
Plaza de Barrio Nuevo
Santo Tomé
Catedral
Posada de la Hermandad
Calle de los Reyes Católicos
Santa Maria la Blanca
Calle de San Juan de Dios
Palacio de Fuensalida
Ayuntamiento
Calle Cardenal Cisneros
Puente de San Martín
Plaza del Conde
Calle Taller del Moro
Sephardic Museum
Calle de Samuel Levi
Calle de Santa Isabel

T O L E D O

Río Tajo

0   200 m

Inset map

Chinchón
Aranjuez
Cuenca
Toledo
Mora
Tembleque
Orgaz
Motilla del Palançar
Consuegra
Madridejos
Belmonte
Alarcón
Alcázar de San Juan

0   40 km

3
From Toledo to Cuenca

Toledo – Orgaz – Consuegra – Cuenca

'A little town, strong because of its situation', is how the Roman historian Livy described Toledo in the first century BC. It stands on the plain of Castile, and virtually the only approach to the city is through a narrow opening in the impregnable, horseshoe-shaped granite hills which surround it, and whose solitude and utter desolation, as Augustus Hare put it in 1873, girdled Toledo from the living world.

Once the capital of the kings of Castile, still the seat of the metropolitan archbishops of the country, Toledo is today quieter than it has been through most of its long history. In AD 418 the Visigoths took the citadel from Rome. Toledo became the Catholic metropolis in 587, when a Visigothic king renounced Arianism for the orthodox faith, and between the fifth and the sixteenth centuries some thirty ecclesiastical councils were held here.

In between, Toledo became a Moslem city. The Visigoths persecuted Jewish Toledans, who in desperation encouraged the Moslems to invade. Legend, of course, tells another story, namely that in the year 711 the last Visigothic prince, Rodrigo, espied a count's beautiful daughter bathing in the gorge of the Tajo. Her enraged father invited the Moslems to aid his revenge. Even today in Toledo you are shown the *baño de la cava*, a spot below the Puente de San Martín, where the exquisite Florinda took her fateful bath.

Moorish rule lasted from 712 for almost four centuries. Initially an emir controlled the city on behalf of the Caliph of Córdoba, but the Arabs of Toledo achieved independence in 1035. Arab rule was for the most part extremely tolerant, and the original Christians, taking up the language of their rulers, were officially dubbed 'half Arabs' (*Mozarabs*) while still being allowed to practise their own religion.

With the help of El Cid, King Alfonso VI of Castile took the city back in 1085. He so liked the place that two years later he transferred his court from Burgos to Toledo. Although Alfonso ordered that the first Mass in his newly conquered city should be celebrated in the superb mosque of Toledo, the Moors were not persecuted. Though they twice (in 1197 and in 1295) vainly besieged the city, their language was banned at Toledo only in 1580. In the words of the English architect G. E. Street, Toledo from the thirteenth century onwards displayed 'a toleration of Jews and Moors, which it would be hard to find a parallel for among ourselves', while at other times indulging in 'intolerance, such as has no parallel out of Spain elsewhere in Europe'. As a result Toledo is a city enriched by Arabic architecture, whose masterpieces include the Taller del Moro, the Casa de Mesa and a superb synagogue. Inevitably, in time some of these Jews and Moors converted to Christianity, and both St

Teresa of Avila and St John of the Cross were descended from converted Jews of Toledo.

Another Moorish legacy is seen in the tortuous narrow streets of the city, which have been preserved for a purely practical reason, to shelter the inhabitants from the winter winds and the pitiless summer sun. Tall houses, windowless on the *calle* side, flank these streets, huge doors opening on to flower-decked patios at the back.

During the reign of the Emperor Charles V Toledo became a leading stronghold of the *comuneros*. Defending the franchises of the common people, they were led at Toledo by Juan de Padilla and, after his death, at the battle of Villalar by his widow María Pacheco (who escaped to Portugal when the city finally capitulated). Toledo was an uncomfortable city for monarchs. Paradoxically the power of the archbishops, who virtually ruled the city for centuries, also ultimately hastened its decline. Their power convinced Felipe II that he had made a serious mistake in transferring his court here from Valladolíd in 1559, and he soon moved to Madrid.

The greatest Christian legacy is the cathedral, which was founded in 1227 on the site of a sixth-century church that had been transformed into a mosque in 712. The Christians took over again at the end of the eleventh century and decided to build anew, this time using a French architect, Pedro Pérez, and building in the French gothic style. The Toledans finished their cathedral only in 1493. Throughout this long period the international contacts of Catholicism continued to bring French architects to this part of Spain, and Toledo cathedral still resembles the gothic ones of northern France.

Flying buttresses support its walls. The south tower was crowned with a cupola by El Greco's son, Jorge Manuel Theotokópoulos. El Greco himself painted one of his two most celebrated altar-pieces, *Jesus being Stripped of his Garments*, for this cathedral. (The other,

Toledo rises above the River Tajo in the late afternoon sun.

The renaissance former Hospital of Santa Cruz de Mendoza at Toledo. This rich plateresque doorway is the work of Alonso de Covarrubias.

The Burial of Count Orgaz, is also in Toledo, in the church of San Tomé).

Three gothic doorways at the west end, built in the first half of the fifteenth century, are decorated with reliefs. On the right is depicted the Last Judgment, while on the left green men sport among leaves. The relief over the central doorway depicts a major event in the religious history of the city, the occasion in December 666 when the Blessed Virgin Mary appeared in Toledo to present St Ildefonso with a chasuble. She was especially pleased with the saint, who was Archbishop of Toledo, for defending the immaculate conception of her son in his *De Virginitate Perpetua Sanctae Mariae*.

Above the relief of the miracle of St Ildefonso is another, depicting the Last Supper. St John sleeps, while at the right-hand side the traitor Judas is seen with a money bag. Statues of prophets, angels and saints ornament the ogival arch of this doorway. Above the side arches are decidedly baroque statues, and higher up is a huge rose window partly hidden by a parapet. The façade rises to a simple classical upper story which was added in 1787.

On the left stands the cathedral's belfry, some 90 metres high, its five lower storeys built by Rodrigo Alfonso and Alvar Martínez between 1380 and 1440. Decorated with colonnettes, ceramic tiles and gothic arches, they culminate in a Flamboyant gothic storey added in 1442 by a Brussels mason, who took the Spanish name Annequín de Egas. His work is topped by a crown of thorns. As for the cathedral bells, the heaviest weighs 17,515 kilos and dates from 1753.

Before going inside the cathedral it is rewarding to walk around it, relishing especially some of its other magnificent doors. The Puerta Llana stands in the Calle Cardenal Cisneros, a narrow alleyway running from the palace of justice. Puerta Llana means 'level door' (simply because no steps rise to it); it was designed in the classical style in 1800 by Ignazio Haám. It looks like the entrance to a Greek temple stuck incongrously on to a gothic church. Beyond it is the resplendent gothic Puerta de los Leones, so named because of the six sculpted heraldic lions which guard it. It was designed in 1460 by Annequín de Egas, and the decoration is by the sculptor Juan Fernández Alemán, who was inspired by Italian models. Above this doorway is a relief added by Eugenio Durango in the eighteenth century. It depicts the death, burial, assumption and heavenly apotheosis of the Blessed Virgin Mary. The magnificent bronze doors were made in the late 1540s by Francisco Villalpándo and Ruy Díaz de Corrál. Baroque portrait busts of saints flanking the Virgin Mary add more detail to this *puerta*.

Beyond the apse of Toledo cathedral rises the fifteenth-century inn (or *posada*) of a sacred confraternity, the Santa Hermandad, set up in the thirteenth

The superbly sculpted west entrance to Toledo cathedral.

Heraldic lions have given the name Puerta de los
Leones to the south portal of the cathedral at Toledo.

century by Alfonso VIII and charged with defending
the little villages in the mountains around Toledo. The
confraternity retained quasi-judicial powers until
1853, and its inn contains both a tribunal and a prison.
Over its doorway are the arms of King Felipe II (carved
in wood) and of the Catholic Kings Ferdinand of
Aragon and Isabella of Castile. We know that medieval
people often felt a justifiable need to defend themselves, but how did anyone manage to reach the door-
knockers high up on the *posada*'s fortified door?

Walk around the apse and the sacristy of the
cathedral to discover, down a little *calle* between the
cathedral octagon and the cloisters, the Puerta del
Relój, an early fifteenth-century gothic doorway
named after the one-handed clock above it. Its ornamental grille dates from 1482. Its decoration includes a
kind of sculpted strip cartoon, which begins at the
bottom on the left with the Annunciation, and follows
on with scenes showing the shepherds worshipping

the Infant Jesus, the Magi following a star to bring him
gifts, and soldiers slaughtering innocents at the re-
quest of King Herod. Then, one line up, the tale
continues, running this time from right to left, with an
angel warning Joseph in a dream of Herod's plan to kill
Jesus, of the Flight into Egypt, and so on. One pleasing
touch is that when the sculptor reaches the scene at
Cana where Jesus turned water into wine, he provides
absolutely huge water pots for the miracle.

Return now to the west end of the cathedral, to the
triangular Plaza del Ayuntamiento. Here Church and
State face each other, for the city hall and the palace of
justice (with an unthreatening gothic portal) stand
across the square from the archbishop's palace, recog-
nizable by the cardinal's hat on its Doric portico.
Though the town hall was built in the fifteenth
century, J. M. Theotokópoulos gave it a classical
façade in the seventeenth. Gómez Manrique wrote a
poem which enlivens the wall of its main staircase,
urging the councillors of Toledo as they ascended to
abandon nepotism, greed and sentimental pity, em-
bracing in God's name only honour.

Inside the cathedral double aisles flank a nave which
ends in a semi-circular apse and a double ambulatory.
Eighty-eight clustered shafts rise to elaborate capitals
supporting the ceiling. These shafts are themselves
supported by corresponding columns in the huge
crypt. The pavement is of black and white marble, and
the whole cathedral is lit by Flemish stained glass
windows, the early fourteenth-century work of Jacob
Dolfin and Joachim of Utrecht, and the early fifteenth-
century work of Albert of Holland.

On entering the cathedral the devout visit first of all
a little chapel set against the second pillar of the north
aisle. The Capilla de la Descensión de Nuestra Señora is
basically a gothic tower, built in 1610 by Gregorio
Vigarni of Burgundy on the spot where the Virgin
arrived in 666 to reward Ildefonso with his chasuble.
She stood on a stone which is today protected by a
grille, though the fingers of the faithful, thrust
through the railings, have deeply incised it. He is seen
here proudly wearing his chasuble.

Half-way up the church is the choir, screened by a

mid sixteenth-century plateresque grille designed by Domingo de Cespedés. The outside walls of the choir have an elaborate renaissance arcade supported on 52 columns of Toledo jasper. Above this arcade are niches which contain reliefs, carved around 1380 and depicting stories from the Old Testament.

Over the altar of the choir is a stone statue of the Blessed Virgin Mary, itself enclosed by a delicate renaissance grille made by Franciso Villalpándo and Ruy Díaz de Corrál in the 1560s. The walnut stalls are magnificent, the 54 carvings on the lower ones completely out of place in a house of God, for they represent scenes from the reconquest of Granada by the Catholic Kings. They were done in 1495 by Rodrigo Alemán. The upper ones, rich in intarsia work and completed in 1543, are (on the north side) by Alonso Berruguete and (on the south side) by Felipe Vigarni.

Berruguete also made the archbishop's throne. Sculpted with the arms of Cardinal Silicéo, it is graced by a canopy borne on bronze columns and topped by an alabaster representation of the Transfiguration on Mount Tabor. Felipe Vigarni's brother Gregorio embellished the back of the throne with another depiction of St Ildefonso receiving his chasuble from the Virgin Mary. The cathedral clergy seated here (on misericords depicting feuding couples, pigs and other rustic scenes) look out on to three lecterns, two of them made by Nicolás de Vergára and his son Juan Corbella in 1570, the third created by Flemish masters in 1525. It depicts a magnificent bronze eagle killing a serpent and mounted on figures of the apostles.

In front of the choir, the altar of the trascoro has a fourteenth-century French statue of the Blessed Virgin, above which is a medallion by Alonso Berruguete depicting God the Father. Flanking this altar are alabaster statues of Innocence and Sin, sculpted by Nicolás de Vergára around 1550.

Beyond the choir, at the heart of the cathedral, is the Capilla Mayor, which stands above the mausoleum of the kings and archbishops of Toledo. It is entered from the north transept, through a plateresque grille made by Francisco Villalpándo in 1560 and lavishly painted in gold and silver. Villalpándo also carved the massive statue of Jesus which towers over it. Above the red and white marble pavement rises a triforium of horseshoe-shaped arches. The statues here include one of Martín Alhaga, a shepherd who in 1212 led King Alfonso VIII and his army by way of a mountainous path to Las Navas de Tolosa, where they defeated the Moorish force of Mohammed en-Nâsir.

The high altar is a magnificently flamboyant gothic fantasy, and backing it is a gothic retable of gilded and painted larch wood, commissioned in the early sixteenth century by Cardinal Cisneros from Pedro Gumíel and the Brussels-born architect Enrique de Egas. Here too is the sculpted effigy of Cardinal Pedro González de Mendoza, another archbishop, who died in 1495 and lies beneath in his renaissance sarcophagus. These men, who headed a private army as well as a cathedral chapter of 158 canons and other clergy, at times virtually ruled Spain, defending her against her enemies. On the right of the high altar are the tombs of Sancho IV el Bravo and Sancho III el Deseádo, and on the left lie Alfonso VII and the son of Alfonso XI, the Infante Don Pedro de Aguilár. Outside this chapel, behind the high altar, is the tomb of Cardinal Diego de Astorga, transformed into a piece of churrigueresque theatre by the marble riot of angels and archangels of the *transparente*, created by Narciso Tomé in 1732. (A *transparente* is an altar-piece or chamber behind the high altar, lit from above by a lantern or a skylight.)

Virtually every side chapel in this remarkable building is worth exploring, if only at a canter. Many of them are screened by superb grilles. Start at the south-west corner with the Capilla Mozárabe, which Enrique de Egas built for Cardinal Cisneros in 1504. Since the cardinal was present when the Castilians captured Oran, a fresco of 1514 by Juan de Borgoña depicts him setting out by ship to the battle and landing at Mers-el-Kebir, while in the centre is the storming of the city. His coat of arms is incorporated in the stained glass of 1513 which Juan de la Cuesta made for the chapel.

The Capilla Mozárabe also has a cupola by the son of El Greco and a grille of 1524 by Juan Francés (or Jean de France), a French genius whose skills raised the art of forged ironwork in Spain to new heights. In this cathedral alone he was responsible for the grilles of the chapels of the Epifanía, the Concepción, San Eugénio and San Martín. It seems hard to believe, but these are not his greatest works; his grilles for the church of San Justo at Alcalá de Henares and for the chapel of Cardinal Cisneros in Avila cathedral are even finer.

To the east from the Capilla Mozárabe is the Capilla de la Epifanía, with a fifteenth-century altar-piece and a gothic tomb protected by the grille of Juan Francés. Next comes the Capilla de la Incarnacíon, whose winged altar painting is also by Juan de Borgoña. As his name implies, Juan was a Burgundian. He had enriched his technique by studying in Italy in the workshops of such masters as Ghirlandaio. Juan was responsible for the lovely scenes from the life of Jesus on the reredos of the next-but-one chapel (the Capilla de San Eugénio). Two tombs in this chapel contrast and yet represent pinnacles of Spanish sculpture: the *mudéjar* tomb of Alguacíl Fernán Gudiel on the right dates from the late thirteenth century, while the alabaster effigy of Bishop Fernando del Castilla was made in the 1520s. The statue of St Eugenius was carved by Diego Copín in 1517.

Just beyond this chapel is a famous monumental fresco of the patron saint of travellers, St Christopher, carrying the Christ child on his back and known as the *Cristobalón*. Long admired by the Toledans, the *Cristobalón* was so faded by the seventeenth century that he was repainted by Gabriel de Rueda in 1638. The next chapel is the thirteenth-century gothic Capilla de Santa Lucía, the patron saint of the blind. In 1592 Domingo de Cespedés made the grille of the chapel beyond it, the chapel of the Holy Spirit (and of the *Reyes Viejos*), and Francisco Comontes made its retables a decade later.

We have almost reached the chapter-house, which is entered by way of the Capilla de San Nicolás. The doorway to this chapel is decorated with three early sixteenth-century statues – of the Virgin Mary, St John the Evangelist and St James the Great dressed as a pilgrim – by Diego Copín.

Then comes a small antechamber to the chapter-house, with a lively coffered ceiling dating from 1549. Ornate and gorgeous ecclesiastical vestments are displayed in this room, as are the elaborate chests in which such garments were kept. A plateresque doorway leads into the main hall of the chapter-house, its splendid ceiling painted in gold, red and blue. But the finest works here are thirteen frescoes by Juan de Borgoña, depicting scenes from the New Testament. *The Last Judgment* covers the wall facing you as you enter, followed by the stories of Jesus's birth, passion and resurrection. Then Juan de Borgoña deserts the biblical narrative to depict the death and assumption of Jesus's mother and her presentation of the chasuble to St Ildefonso. Underneath these scenes he frescoed portraits of the archbishops of Toledo from the earliest times to the present. Some are idealized, some not; some look triumphant, others doleful and anxious. A surprising number survived into their nineties. Diego Copín carved the archbishops' throne in the middle of the chapter-house.

The Capilla de San Ildefonso is at the easternmost end of the cathedral, overfilled with renaissance and gothic tombs and usually packed with worshippers (that is when it is unlocked). One tomb contains the corpse of that brutal advocate of papal power, Cardinal Albornoz, who died at Viterbo in 1364. Next to Ildefonso's chapel is the Capilla de Santiago, with its magnificently arrogant statuary and decorative cockle shells. Dedicated to St James the Great, this gothic masterpiece was built in 1435 at the expense of Count Alvaro de Luna as the mortuary chapel of his own family. Alvaro, master of the order of Santiago, lies here, buried after his execution at Valladolid in 1453, in a tomb made of Carrara marble by Pablo Ortéz. His daughter, Doña María de Luna, commissioned the tomb, along with five others, from Ortéz. She lies in one of them, and in another is Alvaro's wife, Juana de Pimentel. Four knights of Santiago guard the four corners of Count Alvaro's tomb; four Franciscan monks watch over his wife, while her piety is suggested by a serving woman holding a holy book. The enthroned Madonna and St James the Great appear in the reredos of the altar, and the climax of the chapel is a relief of St James in his role as *Matamoros*, slayer of the Moors.

A renaissance chapel, the Capilla de los Reyes Nuevos (the 'new kings' of Spain were those descended from the illegitimate Enrique II, who killed his half-brother Pedro I, el Cruel, in 1369) stands to the north-east of the Capilla de Santiago. Enrique II was entombed here after his death ten years later, and only three years after that his widow Joan was laid to rest alongside him. The bones of Catherine of Lancaster, the daughter of John of Gaunt and wife of Enrique III, also lie here, as do those of her husband.

El Greco painted an altar-piece for the nearby sacristy in which soldiers at the foot of the cross dice for the seamless robe of Jesus. In the same artist's *Apostolado*, or apostle cycle, St Luke has a deathly white face and a green robe, his gospel open with a miniature of the Madonna who is lovingly portrayed. St James the Great seems deeply troubled. Heavenly angels swirl above St Joseph and the Infant Jesus. El Greco's rapturous greens appear again in his portraits of saints John the Evangelist, Andrew and Thomas, but his sterner side comes to the fore in the famous *El Expolio*. His St Peter, who has betrayed his master, is depicted desolated, trying to hold back his tears.

In this same room hangs Zurbarán's severe portrait of the Dominican Cardinal de Cusa, as well as *The Taking of Christ*, showing Judas betraying his master with a kiss, painted by Goya. Just beyond the Puerta del Relój is the gothic Capilla de San Pedro, large enough to be utilized as a separate parish church. Finally, at the far end of the aisle is the cathedral Treasury, housed in the chapel of San Juan and containing a magnificent monstrance, nearly 3 metres high. It was made for Cardinal Cisneros by Enrique de Arfe in 1524, using some of the first gold brought by Christopher Columbus from the New World, and is decorated with 260 silver-gilt statues.

At the north-west corner of the cathedral the steps of the renaissance Puerta de la Presentación of 1568 take you to the cloisters and their pretty garden. Turn back to spy above the arch of the door a relief of the

Toledo's *alcázar* rises above the medieval Alcántara bridge.

Presentation of Jesus in the Temple. Begun in 1389, the lower cloister is frescoed with scenes from the lives of saints. At the opposite end of the walk that runs from the Puerta de la Presentación is the Capilla de San Blas. It was built for Cardinal Pedro Tenorio, founder of this cloister, and after his death in 1399 he was entombed here beneath a monument by Fernán González. Cardinal Cisneros was responsible for adding the upper gallery of the cloister. The cloisters of Toledo cathedral are the home of giant and extremely colourful puppets, representing the four corners of the globe, El Cid and other personages of Toledan history. These come out of doors to be paraded around the streets on 20 and 21 June, the feast of Corpus Christi. Flowers and herbs strew the streets, their gentle charm contrasting with the bullfights which also regale the populace.

Leave the cloisters by the western Puerta del Molléte, from which the poor in former times were fed with the little circular rolls the Toledans dub *molletes*.

The little opening through which the *molletes* were handed out is still there. We are now back on the Plaza del Ayuntamiento, from whose southern corner Calle de Santa Isabel runs as far as the Plaza de San Andrés and the *mudéjar* church of the same name, with its polylobe and horseshoe arches. The former burial chapel of the Fonsecas, San Andrés has gothic tomb niches which contrast with its three superb classical reredoses and the early sixteenth-century paintings above its tiled altars. The nave has a fantastic wooden Mozarabic ceiling. Beside it stands the sixteenth-century *mudéjar* Palacio del Rey Don Pedro. Stroll around the outside of the church to see more polylobe arches and the convent of Santa Isabel de los Reyes.

Walking alongside the cathedral cloister and following the signs for the *alcázar*, you reach Plaza 4 Calles. One of the four streets is Toledo's business centre, though one would never guess it from its quiet, narrow curves and its overhanging balconies. This Calle del Comercio runs as far as the huge, triangular Plaza de Zocodover, whose name derives from *sûkh*, which is Arabic for market. On two sides of the triangle are shops and cafés sheltered by arcades and overlooked by balconied apartments, and market stalls are set out under the trees.

Immediately due south of this plaza, at the highest point of Toledo, is the *alcázar*. On this strategic spot the Romans built their camp, which the Visigoths later fortified. El Cid governed Toledo from this citadel, though its present palatial form derives from later rebuildings, chiefly under Alfonso VIII and Alfonso X, the Wise, who gave the *alcázar* its present aspect of a quadrilateral fortress guarded at each corner by square towers. Distressingly, the *alcázar* frequently burned down. It was set alight in 1710 during the war of the Spanish Succession; the French gutted it in 1808; and another disastrous fire raged here in 1887. During the Civil War the republicans took seventy days of bombardment to dislodge the cadets of the infantry school from the *alcázar*. In consequence it was repeatedly rebuilt – by Ventura Rodríguez in the second half of the eighteenth century, again in the 1860s and subsequently twice more.

It remains, nonetheless, imposing, looking out over the curving River Tajo to wild countryside and hills, and across the city to Toledo's military academy and *castillo*. Alonso de Covarrúbias built its plateresque portal in the sixteenth century at the behest of the Emperor Charles V (whose coat of arms adorns it) and rebuilt its west façade. Enrique de Egas was responsible for the powerful north façade, and Juan de Herrera designed the regal south façade, as well as one of the staircases of its patio, whose double arcade rises on Corinthian columns. Slender gothic arches support the upper arcade, while the double-headed eagle appears in the spandrels of the lower one. A lighter, more charming note is provided by the tiles which embellish its walls.

In the centre of the patio is a copy of Pompeo Leoni's statue of Charles V as victor over Tunis, his foot on the neck of a chained Moor. Its two inscriptions read SI EN LA PELÉA VEIS CAER MI CABALLO Y MI ESTANDARTE, LEVANTÁD PRIMERO ESTE QUI Á MI ('If you see my horse and my standard fall in battle, raise the standard before you lift me'), and QUEDARÉ MUERTO EN AFRICA Ó ENTRARÉ VENCEDÓR EN TUNEZ ('I shall remain dead in Africa or enter Tunis as its conqueror').

Of all the vicissitudes which have befallen the *alcázar* of Toledo over its long history, none has captured the imagination of the Spaniards so much as the seventy-day siege of the fortress in 1936, at the outbreak of the Civil War, when it was held by the supporters of General Franco. One room, the HQ of Colonel Moscardó, military commander during the siege, remains partly in tatters as a result of the bombardment. His telephone is still here, and in four languages you can hear simulated recordings of a conversation he held on 23 July 1936 with his son Luis, a prisoner of the Red Militia. Luis says. 'They are going to shoot me if you do not surrender the *alcázar*'. His father answers, 'Then turn your thoughts to God, cry *Viva España* and die as a patriot'. Luis responds, 'All my fondest love, father', and the colonel replies, 'All of mine to you'. Luis's portrait hangs here today beside that of his father.

When the besiegers realized that in spite of their

numerical superiority the defenders would not capitulate, they resorted to the systematic destruction of the *alcázar* by means of bombing, artillery and mines. The photographs of the ruins when the siege was lifted are moving. Most moving of all are the cellars where 328 women and 210 children lived during the bombardment. Some of the women gave birth during the siege, and the primitive operating table on which they did so is still here.

Leaving behind the dramatic history of the *alcázar*, make your way to the eastern arcaded shops of the Plaza de Zocodover and take the Calle de Cervantes, which runs down towards the River Tajo. On the right is a house in which Cervantes spent part of his life, and on the left a far more imposing building, originally the Hospital de Santa Cruz. It was built by Enrique de Egas between 1514 and 1544 on the orders of Cardinal Pedro Gonzales de Mendoza, whose coat of arms and motto ('Ave Maria Gratia Plena'), carried by two angels, top the superb portal. Above them the kneeling cardinal joins St Peter, St Paul and St Helena in adoration of the true cross, while his attendants take care of his mitre and helmet; like many other cardinal-archbishops of Toledo, Mendoza combined in his own person both Church and State.

Enrique had already built a similar hospital at Valladolid, and these two buildings are gems of early Spanish renaissance architecture. The Hospital de Santa Cruz is designed as a Maltese cross. Beyond the main portal the sculpted inner doorway is plateresque, and the hospital has not one but two patios, each with a double arcade so that inmates could shelter above from the winter cold and below from the summer heat. In the first patio the balustraded staircase has a Moorish wooden ceiling. Oddly enough, the domed chapel of the hospital is gothic.

Today the building serves as a museum, housing for example sixteenth-century Brussels tapestries from the cathedral, which depict the lives of Alexander the Great and the patriarch Abraham. Here too are a Baptism of Jesus by Giambologna and a painting of Mary Magdalene by Sebastiano del Piombo. A whole transept is devoted almost entirely to the works of El

At Toledo the Alcántara bridge bears the city's coat of arms.

Greco and includes an Assumption which he finished a bare six months before his death.

The Tajo is bridged twice on this side of the city, and here too are the remains of Toledo's Roman acqueduct. From the city's Moorish walls (which were reinforced by the walls built by King Wamba in 674) the two arches of the old Puente de Alcántara spring across the river towards the *castillo* of San Servando. As the name Alcántara (derived from the Arabic for bridge) indicates, the first to span the river at this point were the Moors. But the present fortified structure dates from the mid thirteenth century and the late fourteenth. On the west tower of 1484 is a statue of St Ildefonso by

87

Berruguete, for the city needed spiritual as well as physical strength to defend itself against its enemies.

Alfonso V built the *castillo* as a further protection and Alfonso VII reinforced it. Beyond it, north-east of the railway station, are the remains of a Moorish castle known as the Palacio de Galiena. Galiena was the mythical daughter of a mythical king Galafré, and no one would repeat the tale that her father built her this castle were it not referred to by Sancho Panza in *Don Quixote*.

From the northernmost point of the triangular Plaza de Zocodover, Calle Armas leads into Calle Venancio González, along which you wend your way to the *mudéjar* Puerta del Sol. Flanked by towers, this horseshoe-arched defensive gateway dates from around 1100. At the beginning of the fourteenth century the knights hospitallers further strengthened the gate, adding two towers, one semicircular and one square and crenellated. Its decorations include reliefs of the Virgin Mary presenting the chasuble to Ildefonso, St Ferdinand, king of Castile, dispensing justice, and some figures which evidently derive from a fourth-century Christian sarcophagus.

Just below the Puerta del Sol is the spot where El Cid's horse knelt before the mosque of Bâb al Mardom when the champion and Alfonso VI were entering Toledo. The mosque is now the church of El Cristo de la Luz. Alfonso is said to have broken open part of the wall of the mosque and discovered a Crucifix and a lamp – still alight – which had belonged to an ancient Visigothic church built on this site. Triumphantly the king ordered the first Mass celebrated in the conquered city to be said in the mosque.

Whatever the truth of the legend, an inscription on the church façade claims it was built in 922 by the Muslims, who incorporated columns from the former church. And the horseshoe arches, arcades and windows in this church undoubtedly resemble those of the mosque at Córdoba. Beyond the Puerta del Sol, Calle Reál del Arrabál winds as far as the church of

The complex *mudéjar* Puerta del Sol, Toledo.

Santiago del Arrabál, another *mudéjar* building with a Moorish tower, the oldest part of the church, and a lavish façade. Santiago del Arrabál was founded in the late eleventh century, when Moorish architects were happily employed by Alfonso VI who had just taken the city. Built of grey brick with polylobe and keyhole arches, the church was enlarged two centuries later, and its interior decorations date from 1790.

Even where Arabic architecture is no longer in evidence, the Arab language still influences the names of Toledo's streets and buildings. The gateway beyond the church of Santiago del Arrabál is known as the Puerta Nueva de Bisagra, and Bisagra is thought to derive from *Bab Shakra*, the Arabic for a red gate. It was built in the reign of the Emperor Charles V and is emblazoned with his double eagle. His statue dominates the courtyard here, along with a little statue of a bishop. The statue on the gate is Berruguete's depiction of St Anthony. A genuine Arab gateway stands nearby, the Puerta Vieja de Bisagra, still looking much as it did in the eleventh century, when it was built to pierce the Moorish walls of Toledo. Just outside this gate rise the grey bricks and polylobe and keyhole arches of the church of Santiago.

Running through a formal garden is Paseo de Merchán, with its fine views of the city walls. It leads up to the massive Hospital de Tavéra, a renaissance building begun by Bartolomé Bustamente in 1541. Alonso Berruguete designed its main portal, which opens into a colonnaded patio with a double row of galleries, the upper one, in the Ionic style, rising from the Doric colonnades of the lower gallery. Under the dome of the chapel is Berruguete's remarkable tomb of the founder, Archbishop Juan de Tavéra, a monument which shows how much the sculptor had imbibed of the mannerism of Michelangelo. He modelled the archbishop's face from a death mask and covered the sarcophagus with bas-reliefs.

North of the church is Toledo's bullring. To see the remains of the Roman amphitheatre you need to walk through the grid-pattern streets of the suburb to the south-west of the hospital. From the theatre, Paseo del Circo Romano leads directly to the sanctuary of El

The *mudéjar* architecture of the church of Santiago del Arrabál, Toledo. Note the distinctive keyhole arches of the tower.

Cristo de la Vega, for which Berruguete sculpted a classical statue of St Leocadia, for she was martyred on this spot. The first church, built in the fourth century, was destroyed by the Moors and the present one dates from the twelfth century.

You can now wend your way back south-east to the city walls and re-enter Toledo by way of the powerful Puerta del Cambrón, which was built by Alfonso VI in 1102 and rebuilt in 1576. Ahead is the plaza and spiky gothic dome of the church of San Juan de los Reyes. Here in 1476, having defeated the Portuguese at Toro, the Catholic Kings founded a convent and church which they intended as their mausoleum. Their first architect was the Flemish Juan de Guas. Ferdinand and Isabella abandoned their plans to be buried here after they had captured Granada in 1492, but their coat of arms and their initials, F giving rise to Ferdinand's symbol of arrows (*flechas*), Y to Isabella's yoke (*yugo*),

are sculpted on the main entrance, together with a statue of the patron, St John the Baptist. Soon the Toledans had taken up the habit of hanging on the walls of this church chains from which Christians had been released after being rescued from the Moors. A multitude of chains still hang here, so that the building resembles a vast house of correction.

The coat of arms and initials of the Catholic Kings also appear repeatedly inside the church. Its single nave is richly decorated, inscribed with gothic messages, interlaced with arabesques and emblazoned with the coats of arms of Castile and Aragón. Its cloister is a flamboyant gothic masterpiece, the upper gallery with a coffered ceiling. Four sculpted groups and twelve painted scenes decorate the renaissance reredos. The convent is now the provincial museum, among its treasures a view of Toledo by El Greco. Over its entrance is sculpted a cross flanked by figures of St John and the Blessed Virgin, and above the cross a pelican symbolizes Jesus offering his own flesh for his fellow men and women.

The convent is close by the walls of the city and the most powerful of the bridges across the Tajo, the Puente de San Martín. Built in 1212 and renewed in 1390, its five arches are defended by a couple of fortified gateways. South-east of the convent rises the thirteenth-century Santa María la Blanca. This was once the Jewish quarter of Toledo and Santa María la Blanca its oldest synagogue. Founded around 1180, it was transformed into a church in 1405 and later became a refuge for reformed prostitutes. Jews, Christians and prostitutes all benefitted from the skills of the Arabs who built it, for the interior is a delicious example of *mudéjar* architecture. Twenty-eight horseshoe arches rise from the carved capitals of octagonal piers decorated with glazed ceramics, while Arabic motifs enhance the spandrels.

Calle de los Reyes Católicos runs south-east from this church, crossing the Plaza de Barrio Nuevo to reach the synagogue of El Tránsito, which is now the Sephardic

Below Toledo the Río Tajo flows past a ruined bridge.

The gothic lower cloister of the convent of San Juan de los Reyes, Toledo.

Museum. Samuel Levi, treasurer to Pedro el Cruel, commissioned Meïr Abdeli to build it in the 1360s, and it remained a synagogue until the Catholic Kings expelled the Jews in 1492. It was then made over to the knights of Calatrava, and later still was consecrated to the death or 'falling asleep' (*tránsito*) of the Virgin. In spite of these vicissitudes, the interior of El Tránsito has managed to retain the Hebrew inscriptions on its frieze. Beside it, up the narrow Calle de Samuel Levi, stands the house and museum of El Greco. Almost certainly the artist and architect made his home in a house built, like El Tránsito, for Samuel Levi. In truth there are few original works by El Greco inside the museum, but reproductions and the work of other Toledan artists make it well worth a visit.

To see one of his most stunning works, you need only walk north from here along Calle de San Juan de Dios to the church of Santo Tomé, another former mosque. Although this early-fourteenth-century

Mozarabic church was rebuilt in the classical style in the eighteenth century, the tower retains its old lines. Don Gonzalez Ruíz de Toledo, Count of Orgaz, who paid for the medieval rebuilding, died in 1323, and it was reported that both St Stephen and St Augustine put in an appearance at his funeral. Inside the church is a painting of 1584 in which El Greco depicted the event, *The Burial of the Count of Orgaz*. He also depicted himself with a greying beard and black hair, the sixth spectator from the left; his young son, dressed in black, points wonderingly at the miraculous scene in which Stephen and Augustine help the noble mourners to lower the count into his grave. Augustine wears a magnificent cope and mitre of the kind worn by archbishops of Toledo in El Greco's own time, while on Stephen's chasuble is embroidered the scene of the saint's own stoning.

Count Orgaz was noted for his charity. In his will he left for the poor of the city an annual gift of two sheep, sixteen hens, two barrels of wine, two consignments of firewood and numerous sums of money. Above the scene of his interment, the soul of this good man appears in heaven before his judge, bolstered by the intercessions of St John the Baptist, St Peter and the Blessed Virgin Mary. Among the heavenly host El Greco has included portraits of Noah and David.

In Plaza del Conde, close by the church of Santo Tomé, stands the fifteenth-century palace of the counts of Fuensalida, where the Empress Isabella died in 1539. The pillars of its late fifteenth-century patio are *mudéjar* in design. Part of the building is now a bar and restaurant, set beneath the stone arches of the ground floor. And east of the palacio, on the way back to the Plaza del Ayuntamiento, rise the remains of the splendidly decorated fourteenth-century Taller (or 'workshop') del Moro, the longtime base of the masons who built Toledo's cathedral.

The exquisite interior and horseshoe arches of Santa María la Blanca, modelled on Arabic forms though built for the Jews of Toledo in the thirteenth century.

A statue in the palace gardens at Aranjuez.

El Greco himself lies buried a little further north from Santo Tomé, in the classical church of Santo Domingo el Antiguo, where you can also see some of the earliest works he painted on his arrival at Toledo in 1577, a legal document bearing his signature, the last will and testament of Pedro el Cruel and a retable behind the high altar by El Greco's son Jorge Manuel. Born in Crete in 1541, the artist died at Toledo on 6 April 1614. As his parish priest recorded, 'He left no will. He received the Last Sacrament. Buried in Santo Domingo el Antiguo. God watch over him.'

Toledo is the perfect starting point from which to explore north and south-east Castile. First, however, spare time to visit the superb fortress built between 1444 and 1464 by Don Pedro López de Ayala at Guadamur, south-west of the city, which has already been mentioned in the introduction. Then drive north-east along the valley of the Río Tajo to discover the complete antithesis of a Spanish castle, the magnificently cold Herreran palace of the well-watered and wooded city of Aranjuez. Once a royal hunting lodge, the palace was enlarged by Herrera and Juan Bautista de Toledo for Felipe II. Part of the palace was rebuilt by Pedro Caro in the first half of the eighteenth century after some disastrous fires in the 1660s, and the interior décor and magnificent furnishings were provided by Queen Isabella II in the nineteenth century. Her historical tastes are best revealed in a room which copies the Arabic Sala de las Dos Hermanas of the Alhambra at Granada, and in the Saleta de Porcelana, covered with ceramics decorated with oriental motifs.

The gardens are as luxurious as the palace, and include a parterre created by Étienne Boutelou in 1746 and the Jardin de la Isla, a walled park on an island formed by a canal and a loop of the Tajo, which was laid out in 1669 by Sebastián Herrera. Not content with one royal palace, Aranjuez also boasts the Casa del Labrador, which was modelled on the Petit Trianon, Versailles, by Gonzáles Velázquez for King Carlos IV.

Set among olives and vines, Chinchón stands 25 kilometres further north-east. Its glory is a circular Plaza Mayor, from the balconies of whose arcaded three-storey houses the citizens would once watch religious processions and bullfights, as well as the plays of Lope de Vega performed in the open air. The square is still the venue, on the Saturday before Easter, of thé *Pasión de Chinchón*, when the citizens enact the sufferings of Jesus. The feast of San Roch is celebrated every year on 16 August. Although the former Augustinian convent, built in the seventeenth century, is now a National Parador, the sixteenth-century church of the Asunción still functions as a house of God and displays inside an Assumption of the Blessed Virgin painted by Goya.

South-east of Toledo are the lime-washed walls of Orgaz, whose ochre-coloured church is one of the last works of Alberto Churriguera, and unusually re-strained for him. The town is dominated by the fifteenth-century fortress of the counts of Orgaz. Another fortress, given as dowry to Alfonso VI when

Olives and distant hills north of Chinchón.

Above **The arcades of the Plaza Mayor at Tembleque.**

Right **A classic Quixotic windmill near Consuegra.**

he married the Moorish princess Zaïda, rises on a rocky perch just outside Mora, which lies 10 kilometres north-east. This is the setting, during the last weekend of May, of an annual festival of olives. The gothic-*mudéjar* church dates from the fifteenth century. From here the road continues east to Tembleque, another little town with a fine Plaza Mayor, this one built in the mid seventeenth century with a contemporary Casa Consistoriales (town hall). Here again the parish church was built in the fifteenth century.

From Tembleque a major road runs due south through the unwelcoming *meseta*, or plateau, of La Mancha to Madridejos. Consuegra (where I have already surmised that Don Quixote tilted at windmills) lies on the Río Amarguillo, 7 kilometres west through saffron country. It is protected by the remains of a fortress which the Order of St John of Jerusalem built on its ridge in the twelfth century, and which today is surrounded by windmills. The town slopes down the ridge, with the mid sixteenth-century church of San Juan peering across the river at the Ayuntamiento, which was built almost exactly a hundred years later. Here is a late sixteenth-century Carmelite convent and a mid seventeenth-century Franciscan convent, while the imposing dome of Santísimo Cristo de la Vera Cruz rises from a church built between 1750 and 1803. Naturally Consuegra has a saffron festival, on the last weekend of October.

Alcázar de San Juan lies among the vineyards of La Mancha east of Madridejos. It derives its name from a Moorish fortress transformed into the *torreón* of Don Juan of Austria in the seventeenth century, and from the Knights of St John of Jerusalem who protected the town in the twelfth century. Next to the *torreón* stands the romanesque sandstone church of Santa Marìa.

A landscape of vines and windmills is now traversed by the N420, which passes the ruined fortress and Mozarabic church of Mota del Cuervo to reach Belmonte. Here white houses, some of them of consider-

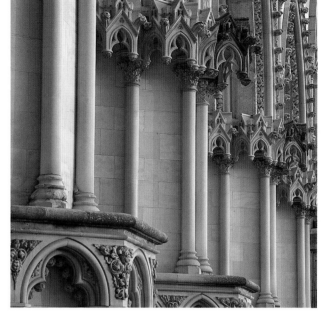

Gothic details from the façade of Cuenca cathedral, which has a surprisingly north European feel.

able pretension, are powerfully defended by a medieval wall and the castle which Juan Fernández Pacheco, marquis of Villena, built in 1456. Belmonte has a gothic collegiate church, the gift of the same marquis, housing the mausoleum of his family. The eighteenth-century reredos, though lovely, is outclassed by some mid sixteenth-century choir stalls which were brought here in the eighteenth century from Cuenca cathedral. Luis de León, poet and monk, was born here, and his family chapel in the church has a plateresque reredos.

Still further east across the Sierra de la Villa, Alarcón – whose name derives from the Moorish *atalaya*, which means watchtower – has a fortress overlooking the Río Júcar. One of the finest specimens of Spanish military architecture, this thirteenth and fourteenth-century castle has been transformed into a National Parador. Along with medieval walls, it protects a town with a renaissance Plaza Mayor. The church

Dawn light softens the formidable aspect of the fortress at Alarcón.

This scowling mask scarcely welcomes travellers to drink from a fountain near Cuenca cathedral.

of Santa María has a plateresque doorway opening into a nave with a sixteenth-century reredos by Alberto Berruguete.

At Motilla del Palancar, 16 kilometres to the east, is a baroque church with a sumptuous baroque reredos. Here you turn left along the N320 for Cuenca. Ruggedly perched amid mountains and set among bizarre rocky outcrops, caverns and massive, isolated boulders, the quiet, narrow streets of the city contrast with the grandeur of their surroundings. Many of the houses are ornamented with the coats of arms of those who once lived in them. In the ninth century the Arabs treasured the site, building here a fortress which they named Conca. The watchtower of their castle survives as the Torre de Mangana, reduced these days to the less demanding task of carrying the municipal clock.

The poplar-shaded Huécar, a tributary of the Río Júcar, leaves its parent to encircle the city on the eastern side, providing the local restaurants with the trout that are such a welcome change from lamb tripe and stewed lamb. Having regaled themselves with fish and meat dishes (perhaps a spicy pig's liver), the people of Cuenca finish their meal with an *alajú*, a sweet made of rosemary honey, nuts and bread-crumbs, lingering over a *resoli* liquer made of eau de vie, coffee, essence of orange, sugar and cinnamon.

Small wonder, fed on such lively fare, that in Holy Week they tend to take the religious celebrations to excess, sounding off ill-tuned trumpets on Good Friday, beating drums and joining in the mocking of Jesus indulged in long ago by the Jerusalem mob. The next day the hooded penitents carry their heavy tableau through the streets.

In front of Cuenca cathedral you find yourself architecturally transported from Spain to Normandy, or even to Great Britain. This is surely an Anglo-Norman cathedral, the upper arches of its façade even open to the skies like the half-desecrated church of Saint-Jean-des-Vignes at Soissons in northern France. The façade was not always like this. Its tower collapsed at the beginning of the twentieth century and has never been rebuilt. In the middle of the rose window the crucified Jesus is depicted in stained glass. Below it three gothic-arched doorways match the arches of the upper storey, the niches flanking them today devoid of statues. St Julián presides over the upper storey.

Cuenca cathedral was begun in the late twelfth century and finished in the next. Its three aisles widen into five as you approach the transepts, and the double ambulatory clearly mimics that of the cathedral of Toledo. The eighteenth-century high altar and stone reredos, the work of Ventura Rodríguez, are protected by a grille by Sancho Muñoz dating from 1557.

The iron railings of the choir were made by Hernando de Arenas in the mid sixteenth century. An aged José de Churriguera contributed the reredos, and the walnut stalls date from the eighteenth century. The

High above the Río Huécar a splendid renaissance doorway beckons visitors into the gothic convent church of San Pablo.

north transept is embellished by the renaissance Arco de Jamete (so-called because its architect was Esteban Jamet, who came from Orléans), built in 1546; Corinthian capitals surmount its fluted columns. Ventura Rodríguez designed the vaults of the chapter-house, whose doorways are by pupils of Alonso Berruguete. The statues here include two superb sculptures by Pedro de Mena, a Mater Dolorosa and another statue of the Virgin Mary.

Explore the side chapels and you will discover behind the ambulatory the Capilla de los Caballeros, whose gothic grille encloses fifteenth-century gothic tombs, as well as a Crucifixion, a Pietà and an Adoration of the Magi, all painted by Fernando Yáñez de la Almedina. In this chapel the most bizarre tombstone is that of Teresa de Luna, who died in the fourteenth century. Her effigy seems to have been flung into a bath of concrete, only her wimpled face and her gloved hands appearing above the surface.

The Capilla de Santa Elena, whose grille dates from 1577, has a sixteenth-century walnut reredos, and the Capilla del Socorro a gothic retable which enshrines a fifteenth-century statue of the Madonna. Behind the high altar is the renaissance Capilla del Espíritu Santo, again crammed with tombs, of which the finest to my mind is that of Cardinal Mendoza, who died in 1586. Seek out the altar of St Julián, dating from 1743 and known as the *transparente* because of the skilful play of light on its jasper, marble and gilded bronze, again the work of Ventura Rodríguez. Look out too for the Capilla del Corazón de Jesús, whose coffered ceiling is another *mudéjar* treat and whose early sixteenth-century paintings are by Jan Gossaert. The plateresque chapel of San Antolín is to be found in the right-hand aisle beyond the transept.

Andréa Rodi and Andrés de Vandelvira built the renaissance cloister of this cathedral between 1577 and 1583. The cathedral includes among its treasures two paintings by El Greco (of Jesus in the Garden of Gethsemane and Jesus carrying his cross), a gilded and silvered fourteenth-century Byzantine diptych and some sumptuous Flemish tapestries.

Apart from the Torre de Mangana, the artistic legacy of the Arabs includes the stuccoed *mudéjar* ceiling of the romanesque-gothic church of San Miguel. Four other churches add lustre to this part of the city: the octagonal seventeenth-century church of San Pedro, opposite the ruins of the turreted *castillo* which was once a fortress of the Inquisition; the baroque church of San Felipe, which was built in the lower city in 1739; an elliptical convent, Las Petras, designed by Ventura Rodríguez; and the renaissance church of La Mercad, which rises in front of a seventeenth-century seminary. Across the River Júcar stands the early sixteenth-century church of Nuestra Señora de la Luz, which houses the statue of Our Lady of the Light, patroness of Cuenca.

Cross the River Huécar by the sixteenth-century Puente de San Pablo to reach the convent and late gothic church of San Pablo, which was built in 1523. In a breathtaking position overlooking the Huécar gorge, the church affords a superb view of a unique feature of the city of Cuenca: the extraordinary fourteenth-century *casas colgadas*, a series of houses which hang perilously over the gorge of the River Huécar.

The *casas colgadas* ('hanging houses') of Cuenca; in one of them is the Museo de Arte Abstracto Español.

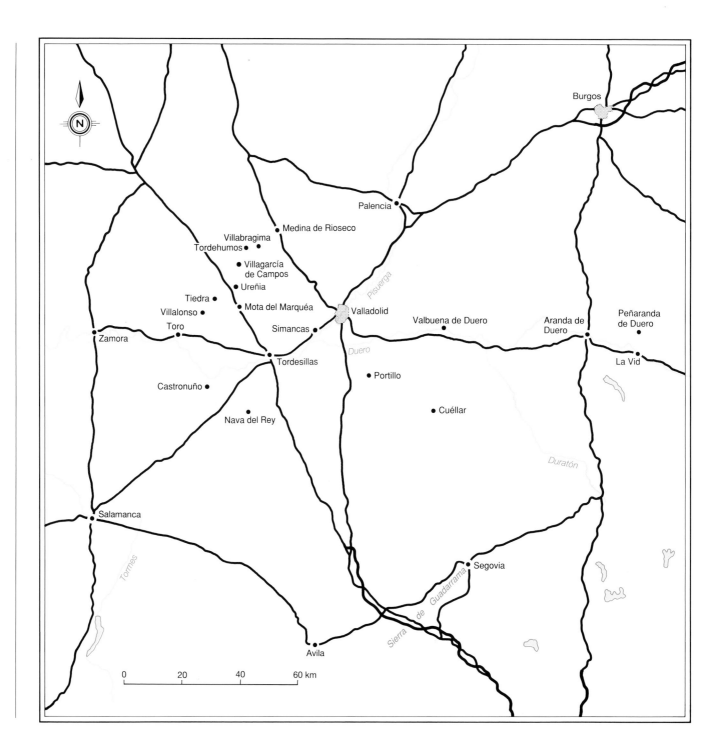

4
From Valladolid to Zamora

Peñaranda de Duero – Valladolid – Toro – Zamora

West of Valladolid is a cluster of attractive towns and villages. One is Peñaranda de Duero, where a cross, to all appearances a religious symbol, stands at the centre of the Plaza Mayor. In fact it symbolizes the fragile nature of citizens' rights in medieval Castile: a late gothic pillory, it was set up here as a warning to any commoner who might feel ready to assert his rights to certain liberties. As a further warning, a fortress, whose ruins still preserve its square keep and crenellations, dominates the tiny town.

This medieval brutality is belied by the gentle aspect of the half-timbered and arcaded houses of the Plaza Mayor. Close by stands an equally civilized edifice, the splendid renaissance Palacio de los Condes de Miranda, built in 1536 by Francisco de Colonia. It has a two-storey inner courtyard with an elegant grand staircase and a wealth of *mudéjar*, gothic and Italianate decoration. Though gothic in style, the collegiate church of the town was finished only in 1732. In the Calle Reál you can visit a seventeenth-century pharmacy whose medical instruments and ceramic pots are in pristine condition.

South of here, on the left bank of the Río Duero, stands the splendid church of Santa María de La Vid (St Mary of the Vine), with a sumptuously decorated sixteenth-century lantern, a choir with baroque stalls carved in walnut, a library of some 40,000 volumes and splendid gothic cloisters. The interior of the church is further enriched by an iron grille wrought by Juan Rodríguez in 1594. The stone statue of Nuestra Señora de La Vid carrying the Infant Jesus, chiselled and painted in the fourteenth century, is enshrined in a renaissance reredos of 1592.

Aranda de Duero, 18 kilometres further west, is a largely modern town of some 27,000 inhabitants, but its church of Santa María la Reál is worth a visit simply for its rich plateresque façade, bearing the insignia of Ferdinand and Isabella. Built by Simón de Colonia, father of Francisco, the church has a renaissance pulpit by Juan de Juni. Peñafiel, which lies south-west along the N122, is noteworthy above all for its magnificent romanesque castle. Built by the Arabs, it was enlarged by the Christians, particularly the Infante Juan Manuel, in the fourteenth century. Dominated by a keep and protected by thirty towers, its dimensions are extraordinary – stretching for 211 metres, it is no more than 23 metres wide.

Of Peñafiel's two major churches, San Miguel is built in the Herreran style (possibly by Juan de Herrera himself) and its sternness contrasts with the plateresque and *mudéjar* exuberance of San Pablo, built of brick in 1324 and decorated with polylobe and horseshoe windows and blind arcades. Peaceful windmills line the Río Duratón as it runs through the town,

At Peñaranda de Duero the medieval pillory stands in front of a gothic collegiate church.

interior was transformed in more peaceful centuries into a less warlike place. Bulls are tormented at Cuéllar at the end of August, during the feast of Nuestra Señora del Rosario, though here they are given a more sporting chance by being allowed to run wild through the town.

From here the N601 takes you north-west to Valladolid, through a landscape of limestone ridges and fields occasionally peopled by shepherds in ponchos guarding huge flocks of sheep. The route passes by Portillo, another hill town, whose fifteenth-century limestone *castillo* has turrets at the corners and machicolated walls. The church of Santa María at Portillo has a decorated tower on top of a square belfry. As fine as both is the superb view from here over the valley, and the citizens have kindly provided seats overlooking it.

Whereas such great Castilian cities as Salamanca and Toledo lie in the most arid of landscapes, Valladolid, though some 2000 metres above sea level, is set on the left bank of the River Pisuerga, at its confluence with the River Esgueva, on a fertile plain known as the *meseta central*. Stretching to the north of the city, the Tierra de Campos produces abundant corn and is dotted with churches, monasteries and castles. Here too are vineyards (the light red wines are especially reputed). More cornfields sprout to the south of Valladolid, and others extend as far as the distant Sierra de Guadarrama. Around Olmedo, still further south in the province of which Valladolid is capital, grow occasional pines. And the neighbourhood of Castronuño and Nava del Rey is covered in vineyards.

Alas, Valladolid itself has been spoiled by urban blight, and to enjoy its treasures you must often thread your way through with eyes closed. If you enter from the direction of Madrid, some 200 kilometres distant, the three arches of the Puerta del Carmen open on to a convent built in the classical style for the Augustinians by Ventura Rodríguez in the mid eighteenth century.

while the circular Plaza del Coso (formerly the Plaza Mayor) is the scene of savage bullfights during the feast of the Assumption, which for the sake of them stretches from 14 to 17 August.

A string of riverside villages follows the Duero from Peñafiel to Valladolid. One of them, San Bernardo, just beyond Valbuena de Duero on the north bank, has a magnificent Cistercian monastery founded in 1144 and dedicated to St Bernard of Clairvaux. Its mid twelfth-century church houses baroque reredoses by Pedro de Corrál with reliefs by Gregorio Fernández.

An alternative route to Valladolid is to drive south-west from Peñafiel to the fortified hill town of Cuéllar, with several romanesque-*mudéjar* churches, in particular San Martín and the mighty San Estéban, and an enormous fifteenth-century *mudéjar* castle. Beltrán de la Cueva, who managed to be both a lover of the queen and also the favourite of her husband Enrique IV, built the castle. Towers guard its four corners, while the

This gothic-*mudéjar* fortress was built at Cuéllar for the Dukes of Albuquerque in the fifteenth century.

Freshly picked grapes at Peñaranda de Duero.

Part of it is now a museum housing the most important collection of Chinese art in Spain, with four rooms devoted to the art of the Philippines.

Beside it rises the church of San Juan de Letrán, beyond which are the Paseo de los Filipinos and the Plaza de Colón, with its massive statue of Columbus. On Wednesday 21 May 1506, Cristóbal Colón Columbus died at Valladolid. Rich from trade, and from his claim to a third in gold of all the revenues derived by the monarchy from the island of Española, he died out of favour with the court he had so signally enriched. Wealth was what he lived and sailed for. Of humble and obscure origins, probably the son of Genoese wool-combers, he let slip the revealing remark after the last of his voyages that, 'Gold is most excellent, for he who possesses it may do whatsoever he wishes in the world'.

Taller than the average man, and a sailor since the age of fourteen, by the time he was forty his hair, a rich red in his youth, had turned completely white and his face was deeply lined. He had already been shipwrecked once, managing to gain the coast of Portugal clinging to an oar; he had sailed to Sierra Leone, to the islands of Cape Verde, to Iceland and to England. In 1479, married to a Portuguese woman named Filippa Moniz, he had made his home in Lisbon, living, some said, as a bookseller. Encouraged by the Florentine astronomer Toscanelli, he had also conceived the notion of sailing to India, not east, but westwards.

For this astonishing scheme he needed a patron, applying first to John II of Portugal, next to Henry VII of England and then to the Duke of Medinaceli. The duke referred him to Isabella of Castile. As a result of opposition from her advisers, many of them clerics who could not accept that the world was round, it took seven years before the Catholic queen and her husband were persuaded to support him. Their decree was vague, running, 'We have commanded Cristóbal Colón to set forth with a fleet of three armed caravels as our captain of the same, towards certain regions of the Ocean Sea to perform certain things for our service.'

Early on Friday 3 August 1492, Columbus, commanding the *Santa María*, with his company of 120 men housed in the caravels *Pinto* and *Niña*, set sail from Spain. They embarked from the bar of Saltes, near Palos, a little port not far up the estuary of the River Tinto at the south-western corner of Castile. They sailed first of all to the westernmost possessions of Castile, the Canaries, and then proceeded further west, Columbus falsifying his log to conceal from the crew just how far they were going. But by 10 October there was unrest among the crews. Two days later the lookout on the *Pinta* cried 'Tierra!': the expedition had reached the New World. As he reported to his royal patrons, Columbus had reached a territory 'of a thousand objects of value', a land promising great trade and profit, dotted with huge gold mines as well as producing spices, aloes, cotton and mastic. As for the natives, both men and women went about entirely

Vineyards bask in the early morning light south of Peñaranda de Duero.

naked and unarmed, were intelligent, remarkably timid and 'so generous with all they have that no-one would believe it without seeing it for themselves'.

Columbus returned in triumph, though the *Santa María* had been shipwrecked. After making two more voyages of discovery to the New World and serving for six years as governor of Española, he was sent home in 1500 in chains, accused of maladministration by a new royal governor (an accusation rejected by the Catholic Kings). Finally, between 1502 and 1504, he sailed to the Gulf of Mexico, a sick man with enemies who plotted against him back at the court of Castile.

From Plaza de Colón, Paseo del Campo Grande runs through the gardens of the Campo Grande (a *campo*, or field, because it was once used for jousting whereas now children sail boats and ducks swim on its peaceful lakes). These gardens enclose a few vestiges of a twelfth-century cloister built by the Knights Templar. At the end of the *paseo* you find yourself in the Plaza de Zorrilla, a square named after the nineteenth-century poet José Zorrilla. His bronze statue by Carretero was erected here in 1900, seven years after Zorrilla had died in poverty in Madrid. Here too rise the imposing towers of Valladolid's military academy, in front of which is a group sculpted by Gil Mariano Benlliure.

If you walk to the east, along Calle Miguel Iscar, you come to the house in which Cervantes lived from 1603 to 1606. In the room he used as a study he wrote *El licenciado vidriera* and *El coloquio de los perros*. Today his home is a museum and library dedicated to his memory. Imaginatively filled with sixteenth- and early seventeenth-century furniture, tapestries and carpets, its walls are hung with maps and a painting of the Battle of Lepanto. In this house one can readily imagine the author sitting by the large fireside after a day's writing, waiting for the pot to bubble between the polished firedogs.

If, instead of walking east, you take Calle de Santiago from the Plaza de Zorrilla, you reach the gothic church of Santiago, founded by the Knights of Santiago in 1489. Inside is a dramatic reredos by Alonso Berruguete depicting the Adoration of the Magi, and in the chapel of the Brotherhood of the Seven Words from the Cross is a portrait of Christ said to be by Francisco de la Maza. In the nave of the church is a baroque reredos by Alonso Manzano with statues sculpted by Juan de Avila.

Walk on into the harmonious Plaza Mayor, whose arcades and porticoes date from the sixteenth century for in 1561 a conflagration destroyed the old square. The statue in the centre by Carretero is of Count Pedro Ansúrez, virtual founder of the modern city. Valladolid derives its name from 'Valle Totium', Gallo-Roman for 'valley of the waters'. After it had long been occupied by the Moors (who called the place 'Balad Valed'), Alfonso VI confided its rule to Ansúrez. Thenceforth Valladolid prospered. In the thirteenth century it was a favourite residence of the court, and Ferdinand and Isabella celebrated their marriage here in 1486. The Catholic Kings also set up the Inquisition at Valladolid, and Felipe II made it his capital. Not that everyone flourished here: east of the Plaza Mayor, in the Plaza de la Fuente Dorada, Alvaro de Luna, the sometime favourite of Juan II, was executed in 1453.

Calle Pasión San Francisco Ferrari, on the side of the Plaza Mayor opposite the city hall, leads a few paces west to two fine religious buildings which are now museums. First, the Iglesia de la Pasión (whose baroque façade is by Felipe Berrojo) is now an art gallery, in which hang baroque paintings that have spilled over from the national collection of Valladolid. They include works by the Florentine Vincenzo Carducci, whom Felipe II summoned to Valladolid in 1585 and Felipe III made court painter in 1609. Further on, in Plaza Santa Ana, stands the convent of Santa Ana, with a six-room museum devoted to ecclesiastical sculpture, paintings and liturgical treasures. There are also three canvases by Goya, works by his brother-in-law Ramón Bayeu, a Mater Dolorosa by Pedro de Mena and a painting of the dead Jesus by Gregorio Fernández. The convent was founded by Felipe II, but it was re-endowed by Carlos III who commissioned the Italian Andrea Sabatini to

---

Glazed balconies on the corner of Calle de Nuñez de Arce, Valladolid.

design the present circular building. Across Calle Pedro Niña stands the tower of San Lorenzo.

From the north-eastern corner of the green Plaza del Poniente (along Calle de San Lorenzo), walk to the majestic church of San Benito, which Juan I de Castile founded in 1388 as the chapel of a Benedictine monastery. Its severe fifteenth-century façade, the work of Rodrigo Gil de Hontañón, has a massive, two-storey portico that seems designed more to repel invaders than to welcome worshippers. Inside are cylindrical piers and three polygonal apses. Across the Calle de San Benito to the east of this church is the Casa de Berruguete, another house imbued with the spirit of one of Spain's great sons, the sculptor, painter and wood carver Alonso Berruguete.

To the north is a quarter rich in churches, convents and palaces. The Doric portico of the church of San Miguel opens into a building that houses the tombs, by Francisco de Praves, of the Pérez de Vivero family who founded it. Its chancel has a reredos by Adrián Alvarez. Here too are statues of Mary Magdalene by Pedro de Mena, and of St Ignatius Loyola and St Francis Xavier by Gregorio Fernández.

Beyond the church, on the right and left sides of the Calle Exposito, stand respectively the palaces of the marquis of Valverde and of Fabio Nelli. The former, in the renaissance style, was built in 1503 but restored in 1763. The latter, built at the end of the sixteenth century for a rich Italian banker, is today the showcase of the Provincial Archaeological Museum (though archaeology apparently includes some fine thirteenth-century frescoes). Beyond these palaces rises the convent of Santa Catalina, and next to it, in Plaza de la Trinidad, stands the early sixteenth-century palace of the counts of Benavente.

Calle San Quirce runs west from the Plaza de la Trinidad to a cluster of handsome buildings which include the former royal palace (now the regional Capitanía General), the Palacio de los Pimentel (now the Diputación Provincial) and the fifteenth-century convent of San Pablo. The first of these, the Palacio Real, was rebuilt in 1661, but still incorporates a monumental plateresque staircase and a plateresque patio, which its architect Alonso Berruguete decorated with classical medallions.

Few could neglect the Palacio de los Pimentel which faces the royal palace from the other side of Cadeñas de San Gregorio. Felipe II (only son of the Emperor Charles V, and the unfortunate husband of Mary Tudor) was born in this impressively simple palace in 1527, and in its vestibule ceramics depict his birth, his baptism and his return to Valladolid. The window which turns a corner of the building is a piece of plateresque whimsy.

We owe the church of San Pablo to the generosity of Felipe II, and its superb late gothic façade to Simón de Colonia, who was commissioned by Fr Alonso de Burgos, Bishop of Palencia and confessor to Isabella of Castile. The arches of its portal curve sinuously. The statues and coats of arms above it are sheltered by a portico whose intricately decorated arch is so flattened that it is a marvel it does not fall. Above this arch is a rose window and above that again are three storeys filled with rows of statues and culminating in a pediment ornamented by the massive coat of arms of the Catholic Kings. On either side, just below this façade, is carved the coat of arms of the Duke of Lerma, who restored the church in the seventeenth century.

This complex Isabelline gothic façade is set off by the virtually blank pillars flanking it, whose austerity is matched by the rest of the church's exterior, save for the double apse. Inside, even though the church was altered in the seventeenth century, gothic takes over again, with a delicate vaulted ceiling and plater-esque doorways in the transepts. One of the five side chapels contains a carving of St Dominic by Gregorio Fernández.

Behind the church is the former college of San Gregorio, today the home of the National Museum of Sculpture, which has a late gothic façade as fine as that of San Pablo. Again the work was paid for by Bishop Alonso of Palencia, and the architect of the façade may

As it rises, the flamboyant gothic west façade of San Pablo, Valladolid, grows steadily more complex and intricate.

An old man pulls his beard while an angel rides on his back: a facet of the entrance of the former college of San Gregorio at Valladolid.

well have been Juan Gil de Siloé. A canopy with climbing *putti* over its doorway forms a genealogical tree of the Catholic Kings, whose arms are sculpted here. Inside is a superb two-storey cloister, whose barley-sugar columns seem to spin dizzily. The richly sculpted swags, arches and friezes (which display the bundle of arrows and the yoke of Ferdinand and Isabella) are almost as fine as any of the sculptures on display here. And these are magical, for the college houses the finest collection of sculpture in Castile: three rooms are devoted to Alonso Berruguete – the retable of San Benito el Real, one of his greatest works, can be seen here – while other rooms display the sculptures of Juan de Juni, Diego de Rodríguez, Pompeo Leoni, Pedro de Mena and the rest. Of the work of the Burgundian Juan de Juni, an Entombment of Jesus, carved in wood and painted, is an unmissable masterpiece, and of the next century perhaps the

greatest sculpture is the penitent Mary Magdalene, carved by Pedro de Mena in 1664. Some splendid choir stalls carved in the 1520s by several hands, also for the church of San Benito el Real, are now on show here. The roof of the library is richly coffered, and the magnificent staircase and *mudéjar* panelling are among the finest examples of Spanish early renaissance work.

In the face of this splendour it is easy to neglect the house of the Marquis de Villena, slightly dwarfed across the street, and to the north of the museum the narrow Casa del Sol, with its plateresque doorway of 1640, once the home of the counts of Gondomar. Spare a glance, too, for the church of San Martín, over to the south, by no means the finest in the city, but a thirteenth-century foundation which was nobly re-built four centuries later. And not far away is another easily forgotten spot that is worth a visit. As a plaque on a whitewashed house declares, the poet José Zorrilla was born in Calle Fray Luis de Granada on 21 February 1817, and students of his work can examine inside his letters and manuscripts, piano, paintings and death mask. On All Saints' Day the Spanish still perform his most celebrated work, *Don Juan Tenorio*.

Return to the Palacio de los Pimentel, and from here take a street named after Felipe II to reach the palace of the archbishops of Valladolid, a mid sixteenth-century building whose chapel houses an early sixteenth-century reredos. Paintings by Vincenzo Carducci decorate the staircase to the throne room, and the principal staircase has a spectacular coffered ceiling. A few metres further on stands the late sixteenth-century baroque church of La Vera Cruz. Inside are statues by Gregorio Fernández of the Sorrowing Mary, of Jesus about to be scourged, of his Humiliation and his Deposition from the Cross. They were made to be paraded through the streets during the Holy Week processions which still take place here.

Turn left beyond the church to the cathedral, the work of both Juan de Herrera and Alberto Churriguera. In 1580 Felipe II had charged Herrera to

The severe Herreran façade of Valladolid cathedral.

replace a church built here in the eleventh century by Count Ansúrez. With two such architectural masters, the cathedral ought to be one of the wonders of Spain. Alas, it was never finished. Worse, of the four towers planned by Herrera, the only one to be built fell down in 1841. Yet Valladolid cathedral is by no means without virtues. The octagonal tower has been rebuilt and is surmounted by a statue of a long-haired Jesus. A false balcony divides the façade into two, both halves Doric but the lower one far more rustic than the upper. Niches in the lower façade house statues of St Paul and St Peter, sculpted in 1792. Above, on four pedestals, stand the four Latin doctors of the church, St Augustine, St Ambrose, St Jerome and St Gregory the Great.

This stern classical façade gives entrance to a building whose renaissance choir stalls are not really its own. Herrera designed them for the church of San Pablo. They set off a retable sculpted by Juan de Juni in 1572, again not for the cathedral but for the church of Santa María la Antigua. Herrera used the Corinthian order for the 32 pillars from which he intended great arches to spring, and reverted to the Doric style for the cloisters.

Next door is the Diocesan Museum, whose finest treasure is a silver monstrance, fashioned like a temple and decorated with an engraving of Adam and Eve in the Garden of Eden by the Toledan master Juan de Arfe. South of the cathedral is another of Vallodolid's baroque churches, this one dedicated to the devoted follower of St Ignatius Loyola, St Philip Neri. And behind the cathedral the ecclesiastical architecture of Valladolid instantly perks up again. Beside the Plaza de Santa María, which centres on a statue of Cervantes, rises the church of Santa María la Antigua, the most beautiful in Valladolid. Built in the late eleventh century as the chapel of the palace of Count Ansúrez and greatly altered in the fourteenth century, it retains its romanesque belfry, whose lights, unusually, become simpler as it rises. The rest of the building

The lovely romanesque belfry of Santa Maria la Antigua at Valladolid.

A riotous churrigueresque façade decorates the university of Valladolid, all that remains of early eighteenth-century buildings which were burned down during the Spanish Civil War.

displays the gothic face of the early thirteenth century. Inside, a gothic gallery hangs from the west wall, the piers are round and powerful and the apse is divided into three. Behind the high altar is a reredos of 1556 by Juan de Juni.

The university of Valladolid shades the plaza on the south-east side of the cathedral. At the behest of Alfonso XI, Pope Clement VI authorized its foundation in 1346. The wildness of its baroque façade, created in 1715 by the brothers Narciso and Antonio Tomé, who were pupils of Alberto Churriguera, more than compensates for the sobriety of the cathedral, while a few paces to the north rises the church of Nuestra Señora de las Angustias. Built between 1597 and 1604 by Juan de Nates, it enshrines the acknowledged masterpiece of Juan de Juni, the *Virgin of the Swords* which he painted in 1561. The high altar is the work of Cristóbal

117

Velázquez, and its sculptures and bas-reliefs are by Francisco del Rincón.

In Plaza Santa Cruz, at the south-east corner of the university, is the Colegio de Santa Cruz, which was founded in 1479 by Cardinal Pedro González de Mendoza. He is depicted over the entrance, kneeling before St Helena. Above the scene are sculpted the arms of the Mendozas, as well as those of the Fonseca family and the Catholic Kings. Juan de la Riba and Pedro Puliod began the building in the late gothic style; renaissance arches and Corinthian columns were added, and finally it was given a plateresque façade and a magnificent, three-storey plateresque patio by Lorenzo Vázquez. The college now houses 50,000 volumes from the imperial library, and its chapel is the home of *Cristo de la Luz* by Gregorio Fernández and a Mater Doloroso by Pedro de Mena.

Calle del Cardenal Mendoza runs alongside this college as far as Calle Colón, so called because here is the (rebuilt) house where Columbus spent his last years, and its five rooms are filled with his memorabilia. Shortly after his death work began on the renaissance church of La Magdalena, which separates his former home from the convent of Las Húelgas Reales. La Magdalena was founded by the Viceroy of Peru, Bishop Don Pedro de Lasgasca, and his recumbent figure, the work of Esteban Jordán (who also carved the reredos of La Magdalena) lies on his tomb inside the church. The convent of Las Húelgas is much older, founded in 1282 by María of Molina, wife of Sancho IV. Its *mudéjar* portal is unique in Valladolid Inside are works by Juan de Juni and a bas-relief of the Adoration of the Shepherds by Gregorio Fernández. And on the tomb of the founder is an exquisite alabaster statue.

The remains of Christopher Columbus lie in neither church. In death as in life, Columbus was a wanderer. Buried first in the Carthusian convent of Nuestra Señora de las Cuevas outside Seville, in 1536 his mortal remains were transferred, as was his own wish, to Santo Domingo in Haiti. In 1796, when the French occupied the island, they were reinterred in the cathedral of Havana. Finally, in 1899, his bones were brought back to Spain and two years later placed in the cathedral of Seville. His epitaph reads:

> *A Castilia y Aragón*
> *Otro mundo dió Colón*
> ('To Castile and Aragon
> Columbus gave another world')

South-west of the city, at Simancas, rises another of the remarkable castles that dominate this part of Castile. This one, with its powerful cylindrical towers, belonged to the Moors until the Christians took it in the eleventh century. Alfonso III rebuilt it in château style two centuries later, and today it houses the royal archives of Spain – over thirty million documents in all. A romanesque tower tops the renaissance parish church of the town, which has a reredos by Inocencio Berruguete and Gregorio Fernández. Simancas stands on the right bank of the Río Pisuerga, which is crossed here by a seventeen-arched bridge.

The waters of the Pisuerga have joined those of the Duero before you reach Tordesillas, some 20 km further south-west. The houses around the arcaded Plaza Mayor mostly date from the seventeenth century. Overlooking the fertile Duero valley, the church of San Antolín is now a museum of sacred art, as is the convent of Santa Clara, once a royal palace, built for Alfonso XI around 1350. Its *mudéjar* façade is ornamented with stone and polychrome ceramics and the twelfth-century patio has Arabic polylobe arches. The chapel's superb coffered roof once graced Alfonso XI's throne room, and the Capilla Dorada is decorated with fourteenth- and eighteenth-century wall-paintings. Tordesillas is notorious as the place where Charles V incarcerated his mother Queen Juana for 46 years after her husband's death, on the grounds that she was insane. As no-one was allowed to visit her, the diagnosis could neither be confirmed nor denied.

It was at Tordesillas, too, in 1494, that Spain and Portugal finally signed the treaty which set the

Rising above the rooftops of Simancas is the renaissance parish church with it romanesque tower.

boundaries of the two countries. Head north-west from here to Medina de Rioseco, if time allows taking a detour west to Mota del Marqués to admire the remaining towers of its ancient fortress, the plateresque doorway made by Rodrigo Gil de Hontañón for the church of San Martín and the renaissance palace built by Gil de Hontañón.

A gateway flanked by Corinthian columns pierces the walls of the ancient town of Medina de Rioseco, whose cobbled arcaded streets are lined with old houses, some still supported by wooden pillars and beams. The main street, known here as the *Rúa*, winds as far as the church of Santa María de Mediavilla, which Gaspar de Solórzano built between 1490 and 1520. Its ogival west doorway is an introduction to the superb ogival ceiling, which becomes more elaborate in the sanctuary. As well as the huge classical reredos filling the apse, there are two baroque and four classical reredoses. The far chapel on the left, the Capilla de los Benavente, is an eye-opening churrigueresque masterpiece. Its riotous designs include the story of Adam and Eve, beginning with her creation from Adam's rib and progressing to their temptation by the serpent (who has the face of a woman) and their expulsion by an angel from the Garden of Eden. God the Father supervises the whole tale.

At the other side of the chapel Jesus, standing on a skeleton, conquers death, with his mother and John the Baptist at his side and the symbols of the four evangelists at his feet. The altar-piece is a splendid work by Juan de Juni. Caryatids galore adorn this chapel, which was built to house the tombs of Juan de Benavente and his wife. Juan Gonzalez de Palicios and Diego de Palicios also lie here alongside their wives. A plateresque screen guards the chapel, and another encloses the choir and its baroque stalls.

Medina de Rioseco has two other good churches, the late gothic San Francisco and the sixteenth-century

---

Tordesillas: the convent of Santa Clara, once a royal palace partly built by Moorish architects for King Alfonso XI after he had defeated their armies in 1340.

renaissance church of Santiago, built by Rodrigo Gil de Hontañón, which has a churrigueresque reredos and statues by Juan de Juni.

A picturesque route runs south-west from here to Toro, by way of the walled village of Villabragima, with its renaissance church of San Ginés. Shortly after it, on the right, the fourteenth-century castle of Tordehumos comes into view, and at Villagarcía de Campos is another fourteenth-century ruined castle, a sixteenth-century church and the beautiful, secluded Monasterio de la Espina, a Cistercian abbey founded in the thirteenth century. Then the fourteenth-century castle of Urenia looms on its hill to the left. At Tiedra a walled keep rises on its mound, while another imposing fortress with projecting castellations guards Villalonso, a spot over which the Castilians and the Portuguese fought in the fifteenth century.

A town of cobbled streets set on a ridge above the fertile wine-producing land watered by the River Duero, Toro is dominated by three superb churches. The Puerta del Mercado, a classical gateway topped by a cupola, on which two families of storks now nest, allows you into its arcaded Calle de la Mayor which leads to the half-timbered, brick houses of the Plaza Mayor. Here the Knights of Malta built the romanesque church of Santo Sepulcro, which boasts three *mudéjar* apses.

Plaza de la Colegiata opens out at the end of Calle de la Mayor, and here in 1160 was begun the splendid collegiate church of Santa María la Mayor. Over its main romanesque doorway an arch is sculpted with king-musicians playing medieval instruments (including a primitive squeeze-box), while around another arch angels dance. The church has a sixteen-sided classical belfry, a triple romanesque apse and another sculpted doorway. Inside, cupolas rise from squinches, and narrow Moorish polylobe windows complement blind arcades. As if this were not enough, the Capilla Mayor houses a Flamboyant gothic tomb and in the sacristy is a late fifteenth-century painting known as *Nuestra Señora de las Moscas*.

Beyond the church, Plaza Espolón, which is planted with roses and pines, overlooks the Duero valley,

Left The lines and folds of the dramatic landscape near Velliza.

Above The superb 'Zamoran romanesque' tower of Santa María la Mayor at Toro.

123

where a Roman bridge – much modified in the Middle Ages – spans the Duero. From here you can make out the ancient Roman road flanking the river. Over to the left five round turrets protect the corners of the tenth-century *alcázar* of Toro. Then walk from the Plaza Mayor along a tortuous route which eventually arrives at the partly ruined *mudéjar* church of San Salvador before reaching the convent church of Santi Spiritus, on the outskirts of the town. This fifteenth-century masterpiece, which has a ceiling decorated with ceramics, houses the tomb of Beatriz of Portugal, who died in 1410 and lies here because she married Juan I of Castile. Walk on through the town to find Rodrigo Gil de Hontañón's church of San Julián de los Caballeros, whose doorway is flamboyantly gothic and whose sculpted and painted reredos dates from the seventeenth century.

Another three Toro churches, which anywhere else would outshine every building in town, here simply call on the traveller to pause for a while. Fourteenth-century *mudéjar* San Lorenzo has a late fifteenth-century reredos by Fernando Gallego; San Pedro de Olmo boasts thirteenth-century wall-paintings; and across the river rises the romanesque-*mudéjar* hermitage of Santa María de la Vega, which dates from 1208. The walls of its apse retain some fragments of late fifteenth-century frescoes.

Running west along the Duero valley, the N122 reaches Zamora. Dominating the River Duero, Zamora has always been a frontier town. The Zamorans base their banner on the eight red streamers carried by the herdsman Viriatus, who was traditionally born here. For a decade after 151 BC he managed repeatedly to vanquish Roman legions, until his enemies finally killed him in 139 BC. Then the Romans threw a bridge across the Duero; its replacement, built in medieval times, still serves the city today.

Long a stronghold of the Moors, Zamora was destroyed by Al Mansour in 988. At the end of the eleventh century Ferdinando I took the city and bequeathed it to the care of his daughter, the Infanta Urraca. Both she and El Cid were brought up here, and he is reputed to have been knighted in Zamora, in the church of Santiago de los Caballeros; at its altar he swore fealty to Alfonso VI. Under Ferdinand the upper city was refortified, the present *castillo* being one of three then thought necessary to defend the stronghold. Today's fragmentary ramparts originally ran around the whole city, the huge blocks of stone which make up the surviving gates of Zamora (the traitor's gate, the Obispo gate, the gate of Doña Urraca, the Zambranos gate and the Olivares gate) still witnessing to the medieval need for military might and vigilance.

When Doña Urraca's brother Sancho II besieged the city, he was betrayed and slain outside its walls, leaving as his sole memorial the name of the traitor's gate. Braving the possible assaults of the Portuguese, the early thirteenth-century church of San Pedro de la Nave was built outside this gate. In times of peace the citizens crept out beyond the walls, founding such districts as Espíritu Santo, the Orta and Santo Tomé, and building for them romanesque churches which still stand. Peace rarely lasted long. New ramparts were constructed to enclose the districts of Orta and Santo Tomé. In 1476, during the civil war fought by Ferdinand of Aragón to claim his kingdom, the banner of Viriatus was held aloft at the battle of Toro, after which the Catholic King added to it an emerald streamer in recognition of the bravery of the Zamorans during the conflict. Even so, the loyalty of the Zamorans was precarious, and the city became a stronghold of the *comuneros* in their rebellion against the Emperor Charles V.

Close to the city walls stands the hermitage of Santiago de los Caballeros, a single-nave church with fine romanesque capitals. Along the Calle Largo, however, on the river bank, is another twelfth-century romanesque church, San Claudio de Olivares, which has yet more beautiful sculpted capitals. From the river bank you can admire the seventeen arches of the medieval bridge, before driving up into the city by

---

This ruined monastery church at Moreruela, north of Zamora, was the first ever built in Spain by the Cistercians.

way of the Puerta del Obispo to the city's fascinating and unusual cathedral. On the left as you enter, a cardinal's hat surmounting a curving baroque façade announces the archbishops' palace.

Experts surmise that the architect of Zamora cathedral came from France in the first half of the twelfth century, imbued with the spirit of Poitevin romanesque. His patron was Alfonso VII, who determined to found a cathedral here in 1135. Apart from a few later additions, Zamora cathedral was virtually complete by 1174. In spite of repeated fires and consequent rebuilding, its aspect is that of a twelfth-century house of God totally in harmony with itself.

Beside it stands a powerful romanesque belfry, the lower storeys blank, the upper three with respectively one, two and three openings on either side as they rise. The cathedral's most entrancing feature is its dome, covered in overlapping tiles hung like fish scales, which also betrays a byzantine influence of the kind you can still see in south-west France, particularly in the cathedral of Périgueux (though that had fallen into ruin by the eighteenth century and what we see today is a brilliantly imaginative reconstruction by the architect Paul Abadie). At Zamora the strange dome is genuinely medieval. Four bulbous little cupolas and four pointed arches support it, rising from what appear at first to be simple romanesque stone arches but on closer inspection reveal their playful rhythm.

The north side of the cathedral looks out on to a paved square, at the far end of which rise ancient Doric pillars whose sole function today is to give an air of decayed romanticism to the spot. The entrance to the cathedral is an incongruous seventeenth-century classical portal on this north façade, instead of the more normal three doorways in the west front. The reason for this is instantly revealed inside, for where you expect the west wall to be pierced stand three chapels, each with fine retables. One of these, the

Built between 1151 and 1174, the quaint lantern tower of Zamora cathedral rises above the incongruous classical north entrance.

Capilla de San Ildefonso, built to the designs of Fernando Gallego in 1465, is the most exuberant in the whole cathedral.

Sculpted doorways inside enliven the sombre humour of the building. The choir is protected by a lacy iron grille, wrought in the sixteenth century by Jacques Hannequin. Scenes from the Old and the New Testament ornament the choir stalls, which were sculpted around 1500 under the direction of Rodrigo Alemán. In their details the learning of the renaissance is peeping through, combining the biblical figures with the gods and goddesses of classical Greece, with Cybele and the prophetess of Delphi. More familiar in these stalls are the irreverent scenes common to medieval iconography: a woman riding a man, who crouches on all fours while she hits him with her broom; a fox dressed as a monk and preaching to chickens. In the retrochoir is a painting of Jesus in Glory by Fernando Gallego, dating from the mid fifteenth century.

The preaching desks of the early sixteenth-century Capilla Mayor are made of wrought iron, while its eighteenth-century marble reredos, sculpted by Andrés Verde, depicts the Transfiguration. Also adorning the Capilla Mayor are a thirteenth-century sandstone statue of Nuestra Señora la Calva (calva means bald, and the name derives from her high forehead), whose colours were added three centuries later, and the fifteenth-century gothic tomb of Count Ponce de Cabrera. Other chapels are rewarding, particularly one with a statue of Jesus sculpted by pupils of Fernando Gallego, and the Capilla de San Juan, which houses the Flamboyant gothic tomb of Canon Juan de Grado.

The cloister, which Francisco de Mora built in the seventeenth century after the old one burned down, is reached through the complex, twelfth-century arches of the south doorway of the cathedral. Turn back as you leave to see the statues on this portal: on one side a Madonna with two angels and on the other a couple of apostles. In the south side of the cloister is the cathedral museum, whose treasures include a plateresque monstrance by Juan de Arfe and a group of the Madonna and St John sculpted in Carrara marble by Bartolomé Ordoñez; the unexpected treat, however, is a series of Flemish tapestries from Brussels, some from the fifteenth century depicting the life of Tarquinius Superbus, some made in Brussels a century later and devoted to Hannibal in Italy, and others made for Louis XI at Tournai in the 1460s and illustrating the Trojan War. These tapestries came to Zamora in 1608, donated by the sixth count of Alba y Aliste, whose family palace we shall shortly see.

From Plaza de la Catedral, an arch in the city walls leads to a tree-shaded garden and the remains of the once-powerful *castillo* of Zamora. An abundance of medieval monasteries, now disintegrated, gave rise to the abundance of romanesque churches which still stand in Zamora and are reached today through narrow cobbled streets overlooked by balconies and encased windows. The first, San Ildefonso, is in Rúa de los Notarios, the old street of the notaries, which runs from the east end of the cathedral. Thirteenth-century San Ildefonso was reconstructed in the fifteenth century. Despite this, however, the exterior of the church, and in particular its tough-looking squat tower, whose windows are high enough to be out of reach of marauders, resembles a medieval fortress. The main doorway dates from 1723, the vaulting of the nave has late gothic cusps, and the chapel of the Holy Sacrament has a baroque dome and reredos. In the sacristy is a Flemish triptych given to the church by Charles V. The first bishop and the first archbishop of Zamora both lie in San Ildefonso.

Close by in the same street stands the church of La Magdalena, which derives from the late twelfth and early thirteenth centuries, and combines romanesque with the gothic style. A frieze of sculpted heads in almost perfect condition surrounds the romanesque entrance to the nave, stylized plants adding intricacy to the decoration of this portal. The innermost archivolt is cusped and deliciously Moorish, and surmounting the whole is not a figure of some heavenly being but the grimacing face of a beast. Inside, do not miss two remarkable late eleventh-century tombs, half-romanesque, half-byzantine in style, and be sure to walk around the unusually tall apse of this church,

with its typically tiny romanesque windows. Opposite La Magdalena is the eighteenth-century church of Corpus Cristi, with a couple of sculpted angels over its doorway holding a sculpted Sacred Host.

Calle Ramos Carrión leads from here to the fifteenth- and sixteenth-century palace of the counts of Alba y Aliste, which is now a National Parador. It looks out across a plane-shaded square towards the Diputación, a splendid seventeenth-century pink stone palace. In this square stands a statue of the legendary Viriatus, inscribed with the words TERROR ROMANORVM. Beyond the parador, the bust of Ramos Carrión stands in front of the theatre named after him. A plaque on the handsome music conservatory declares that we are an awesome 652·6 metres above sea level.

Between the parador and the church of La Concepción, which has a statue of the Virgin Mary in a niche over its door, is the thirteenth-century church of San Cipriano, which was founded under Alfonso V in 1025. Its crumbling square tower seems to wear a dunce's cap. Humble San Cipriano overlooks another romanesque building, Santa Lucía, which is set lower down towards the river. Storks have made their home on its simple belfry, which rises to the ground level of San Cipriano, and they stare back unwinkingly at tourists who peer at them from the higher church.

The half-plastered buildings around Santa Lucía bespeak a bygone glory. A more powerful monument stands in the Plaza de Santa Lucía itself. The sturdy stone walls of the Puño en Rostro palace are enlivened by an entertaining conceit: blocks of stone carved like an elegantly twisting rope which encircles the family coat of arms. Above them is a prancing lion. From the south side of the church Calle Zapateria takes you eastwards towards Santa María de la Orta, which was built by the Knights Templars. Two doorways of this late twelfth-century church open out on to its square, one of the portals romanesque, the other teetering over

---

Moorish archivolts and sculpted heads on the late twelfth-century frieze over the doorway of the romanesque church of La Magdalena, Zamora.

into early gothic; and inside, in the chapel of San Juan de la Vega, is a late fifteenth-century painted reredos.

Further down the hill stands the Mozarabic church of Santo Tomé, built in the eleventh and twelfth centuries, while from San Juan de la Vega, Calle de Balborraz climbs back to Zamora's homely Plaza Mayor. The former Ayuntamiento of 1504 has round arches supporting a balcony with flatter arches, the whole enlivened by a couple of gothic openings and the city's coat of arms. Here too stands the church of San Juan Bautista, a bronze knight atop its sturdy romanesque tower. Founded in the twelfth century, the church was gothicized in the sixteenth but still retains its thirteenth-century rose windows and portals, including an early renaissance door. Inside is the romanesque tomb of a knight, who lies bareheaded, a page at his feet looking after his helmet.

At the far side of the square a little street leads to the right to San Vicente, yet another thirteenth-century church, this one noted for its fine romanesque belfry. On the other side of the *calle* the art nouveau Teatro Principal curves around a corner. If you feel like paying another visit outside the walls, continue westwards from here to the battlemented round towers which protect the fortified gateway of Doña Urraca. Just beyond it stands the romanesque church of Santa María la Nueva, which has preserved fragments of romanesque wall-paintings and is also the shrine of a sculpture of the dead Jesus by Gregorio Fernández. Santa María la Nueva was founded in the seventh century, but 500 years later the citizens of Zamora burnt the first building down during their 'trout riots', when the common people objected to the

---

This carved medallion decorates the portal of the Zamora conservatory of music.

privileges of the nobility, particularly their fishing rights. Traces of the older building remain in the form of eighth-century capitals incorporated into its apse.

Otherwise walk from the south side of the church to Calle de Santa Clara, which is now a traffic-free shopping street with splendid façades and balconies. A deconsecrated eighteenth-century church in this street is the home of a little art museum, whose chief delights are two paintings of the 1630s by Vincenzo Carducci, one depicting a Carthusian monk at prayer, the other St Bruno in the desert.

Adjoining this street is the Plaza de Zorilla, a grassy oasis with a fountain in which a naked mother rolls on her back holding her naked baby in the air. And across the square is the Casa de los Momos, whose sculpted façade delightfully mingles gothic with the renaissance. A powerful renaissance central doorway is matched by a smaller one on the left; delicate string courses define the structure of the interior; escutcheons and intricately carved window frames decorate the upper storey. On a coat of arms a couple of alligators snap at an arm bearing a club. The Conde de los Momos built this palace on the remains of the Moorish *alcázar*.

On the right of the Calle de Santa Clara rises the triple-aisled Santiago del Burgo, built at the turn of the thirteenth century, with a Byzantine doorway opening on one side and an elegantly sculpted arch overlooking the *calle* itself. The street reaches the circular Plaza de la Constitución Española, in which stands the Gobíerno Civil. Beyond this slightly pompous building rises the renaissance façade of a seminary, and beside that is the dour romanesque church of San Andrés. Inside, an artesonado ceiling shelters the monument of Antonio Soleto by Pompeo Leoni. I ask myself how such a tiny, compact city can offer such a wealth of architectural delight, and cannot find an answer.

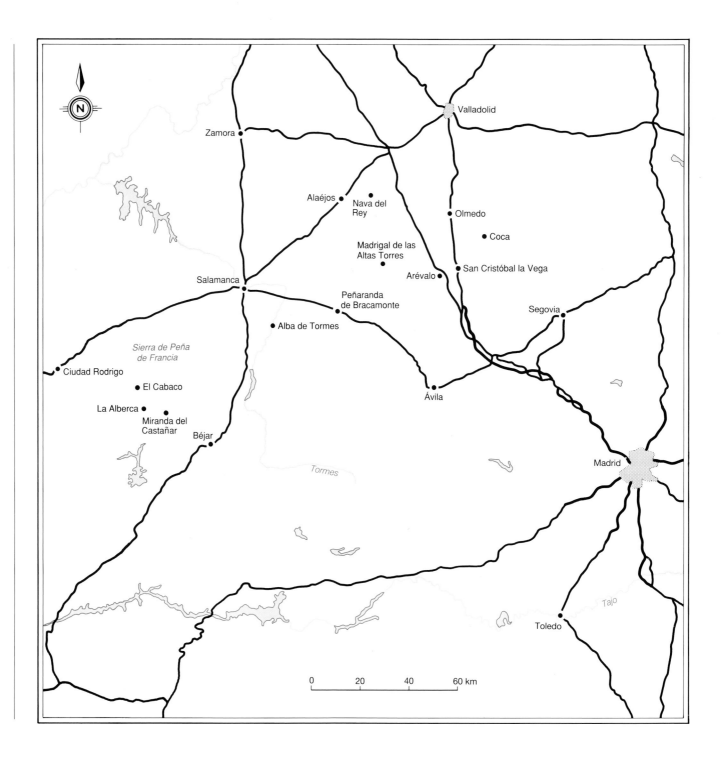

5
From Salamanca to Ciudad Rodrigo

Salamanca – Arévalo – Ciudad Rodrigo

The Plaza Mayor of Salamanca bids fair to be the finest in Spain. Begun in 1729 to the plans of Alberto de Churriguera, it was finished within 25 years by the architect Andréas Garcia de Quiñones. Trapezoidal in shape, it is surrounded by four-storey buildings, the ground floors of which are arcaded. Within the spandrels of the columns are portrait medallions. The south side is occupied by the Pabellón Real built by Churriguera, with its portrait bust of Felipe V who paid for the construction of the square. Opposite rises the Ayuntamiento, whose baroque façade is by Quiñones.

Bullfights no longer take place as they once did in this Plaza Mayor, but the square remains perpetually busy; its arcades and awnings shelter the crowds from the sun – for Salamanca, freezing during the winter, can be unbearably hot in summer.

At the south-west corner of the plaza is a passageway leading into the triangular Plaza del Corillo, where the apse of the late romanesque church of San Martín can be seen. On the north side of the building, over the thirteenth-century doorway, is a relief of the saint himself, along with the beggar to whom he gave half of his cloak. He performs the same act of charity over the renaissance doorway on the south side; to the left the wall of this ancient church seems to be bulging ominously. Hemmed in between the houses on the Plaza de Corillo side is a plateresque doorway dating from 1586. Inside San Martín are seven splendid gothic tombs, two of them under the upper choir, two in the south aisle and three in the north. And the churrigueresque Capilla del Carmen under the choir has a retable sculpted by Alberto de Churriguera.

Calle de Meléndez leads south from the church towards Salamanca's two cathedrals. At the end of the street turn right to Plaza de San Benito, to see the church of San Benito, built in 1104 and rebuilt four centuries later with a plateresque south doorway. Opposite the church a majestic portal opens into equally majestic cloisters, now part of the university.

This whole university quarter is stunningly beautiful. In Calle de la Compañia stands the delightful Casa de las Conchas, which was built in 1512 for Talavera Maldonada, a knight of the Order of Santiago de Compostela, and derives its name from the innumerable cockle shells that decorate its walls and its gothic grilles. This house is rendered all the more charming by its irregularities, for scarcely two of its elegant windows are alike, coats of arms dot the walls, in one case curving round a corner, and the renaissance doorway is set to one side of the main façade. Peer in at the patio, with its vaulted staircase and gracefully curved arches (of a type particular to Salamanca), its carved heads of lions and grotesque creatures and the patterned balcony of its upper storey.

133

In utter contrast to the Casa de las Conchas, across the *calle* is the baroque domed church of La Clerecía, a huge seminary designed for the Jesuits by Juan Gómez de Mora (save for the early eighteenth-century façade, which is by Pedro de Matos). Paid for by Felipe III and his wife Doña Margarita de Austria, La Clerecía was built between 1617 and 1750. The aspect of this seminary is inordinately powerful, even pompous, as if the Counter-Reformation needed proclaiming vigorously even in Catholic Spain. Its façade dwarfs the Casa de las Conchas and still more the little balconied houses beside it. St Ignatius Loyola is depicted on the lower, slightly more restrained façade. The church houses huge gilded baroque retables, some by the Churriguera family. Luis Salvador Carmona sculpted for the church a superb Flagellation of Christ, with angels beside the figure of Jesus bearing the symbols of the Passion.

Alongside the seminary, Calle de Serranos runs on as far as Salamanca's Provincial Museum of Fine Art, which has prehistoric and Roman finds as well as a collection of paintings. Once the home of Alvarez Abarca, personal physician to Isabella of Castille, it dates from the fifteenth century and has a splendid wood-panelled ceiling in one room. Close by, among a cluster of fine buildings, stands the episcopal palace of 1436, the College of San Bartolomé which Diego de Anaya, Bishop of Salamanca, founded in 1401 (though the present building dates from 1760) and the Escuelas Mayores, Spain's oldest university, founded by King Alfonso IX of León around 1219 (as compared with Bologna in 1088, Palencia in 1206, Paris in 1215 and Merton College, Oxford, in 1264). Within half a century of its foundation the Pope had declared it equal in importance to the universities of Paris, Bologna and Oxford. Salamanca university particularly espoused the cause of disseminating Arabic learning throughout Christendom, and students and scholars thronged to listen. Salamanca was also teach-

The Casa de las Conchas, Salamanca: the cockleshells of St James the Great indicate that the house was built for a knight of the Order of Santiago de Compostela.

ing the cosmogony of Copernicus when other centres of learning regarded it as heretical. Here St John of the Cross taught and Cervantes studied.

The university was rebuilt in the first half of the fifteenth century, and fifty years later the Catholic Kings re-endowed it, adding a sumptuous upper storey and the façade in the Patio de Escueles – a plateresque triumph designed in the early sixteenth century by two unknown masters. Medallions, skulls, coats of arms, conches with maidens and bearded warriors, swirls of flowers, branches and fruits, fantastic beasts and ornamented friezes run riot on the wall. Above the central door jamb is a medallion of Ferdinand and Isabella (here called Elisabetha) holding on to their joint sceptre, the king looking quite smug, his hand apparently bestowing largesse, Isabella by contrast placid, her left hand gently placed on the side of the

Salamancan baroque: the Ayuntamiento built by Andrés Garcia de Quiñones rises in the eighteenth-century Plaza Mayor.

medallion. A Greek inscription running around the medallion reads, 'From the monarchs to the university and from the university to the monarchs'.

The coat of arms above the Catholic Kings is that of the Emperor Charles V, with a poor beast representing the Golden Fleece hanging from the bottom of the escutcheon. Flanking this coat of arms are shields sculpted with the crowned imperial eagles, and above these you can just make out Hercules, Venus, the Pope and some of his cardinals. For former scholars, however, all this was as nothing in importance compared to the lucky frog, which sits atop three skulls on the right-hand pilaster. Before an examination the custom was to encourage good fortune by giving the frog a hearty rub.

The university's governing body is still housed in the former Hospital del Estudio, which was built in the late fifteenth and early sixteenth centuries and thus mingles gothic with renaissance architecture. In a patio stands a nineteenth-century statue of Luis de León, in the garb of an Augustinian monk, sculpted nearly three centuries after his death by Nicasío Sevilla. Scholar and poet, Luis de León was born at Granada in 1527, professed as a monk in 1544 and became professor of theology at Salamanca in 1561. He translated the classics and the psalms, but the Inquisition turned on him when he published a translation of and commentary on the Song of Songs. In 1572 he was thrown into prison, but the Augustinian order stood by him and Luis was released four years later. His first words on beginning lecturing again were, 'As I was saying. . .'. Shortly before his death in 1591 the Augustinians made him their superior general.

The Escuelas Menores has a fine plateresque façade with three imperial escutcheons and, over its lintel, the coat of arms of the university. Note too the statue of the great systematizer of Catholic theology, St Thomas Aquinas. Inside is a patio – with a baroque balustrade

A detail of the late fifteenth-century entrance to the University of Salamanca, with, in the lower storey, a medallion depicting Ferdinand and Isabella.

– giving on to a number of rooms, one of which is now an art gallery, with panels by Juan de Borgoña depicting the Annunciation and the Visit of the Magi, and a ceiling painted with the signs of the zodiac by Fernando Gallego. A seventeenth-century reliquary bust contains a relic of Thomas Aquinas. An imaginative seventeenth-century sculpture of St Jerome depicts him busily writing, while nearby one of his relics is contained in an eighteenth-century crimson-painted bust, both portraits giving him a curly beard.

Another magnificent portal with the coats of arms of the Emperor Charles V leads into a double cloister, the upper storey with Salamancan arches (a variant of Moorish arches). Off the lower storey is an eighteenth-century chapel, where the celebrated teacher Luis de León is buried in a marble tomb. In the same cloister is the hall where students crowded to hear his lectures, its original wooden benches and ornate pulpit and sounding board still in place. An impressive staircase rises to the upper storey of the cloister, whose coffered ceiling is by Román Jerónimo. A gothic doorway opens into the great library of Salamanca university, whose 60,000 volumes are housed in baroque bookshelves.

To the west of the university buildings, and divided by the Plaza de Anaya (which was laid out by General Thiébaut in 1811 during the French occupation of Salamanca), stand the old and the new cathedrals. The only way into the late romanesque Catedral Vieja, whose walls are so thick that it is also known as the Fortis Salmantina, is through the Catedral Nueva.

Founded around the year 1100, the old cathedral took a hundred years to build. The interior is enormous and powerful, gothic vaulting rising from the romanesque capitals of the pillars. Capitals, groins and corbels are decorated with a rich array of men, beasts and manikins. The magnificent reredos in the choir consists of 53 wooden panels depicting scenes from the Life of Christ, each one in a gothic frame, by Giotto's pupil Nicolás Florentino. In a tabernacle in the centre of this reredos is an early thirteenth-century copper statue, the Virgin de la Vega, her throne decorated with Limoges enamel. Florentino was also responsible for the great fresco of the Last Judgment on the vaulted ceiling above the reredos. Here an animated Jesus, pointing at the wound in his side, glares at the damned, all naked save for a few hats to identify the miscreants (notably a papal tiara). Angels spin around Jesus, carrying the instruments with which he was tortured and blowing trumpets. The saved, in white robes, rise in orderly fashion while John the Baptist and the Virgin Mary (wearing a ravishing crimson cloak) kneel on either side of the heavenly scene.

As for the decoration of the twelfth-century cupola over the crossing, known as the Torre del Gallo, in the pendentives the angels of the apocalypse call mankind to judgment and on the nearby capitals men wage war.

Steps by the old entrance to the Catedral Vieja lead to the chapel of San Martín and some rare wall-paintings of 1262 which are actually signed, by Anton Sánchez of Segovia. Reds predominate in the frescoes, along with blue-black and white. Jesus displays his wounds in a mandorla over a scene of the Last Judgment, while the man in the moon looks on, along with a fiery sun.

The cloisters were built some ninety years earlier, between 1162 and 1178, and their chief glory is four chapels. The first, the twelfth-century chapel of El Salvador, has an exquisite *mudéjar* vault, and here six times a year the Mozarabic Mass used to be celebrated. This chapel is often called the Capilla de Talavera, for it houses the tomb of Rodrigo Arias Maldonado de Talavera, who died in 1517. In a niche on the right is a romanesque Crucifix.

Dedicated to St Barbara, the second of these chapels was founded by Bishop John Lucero in 1344. This gothic gem is also called the degree chapel, since for many years the university degree ceremonies took place here. The chapter-house, which today serves as a little gallery of religious art, then intervenes, followed by the third chapel, the gothic Capilla de Santa Catalina, with reading desks, splendid reredoses of St Hubertus and St Catherine and a portrait of Don Francisco de Liebana, founder of the president's chapel in the new cathedral. Last comes the Capilla de San Bartolomé, which Bishop Diego de Anaya founded in

1422 and which today contains his own alabaster tomb, the work of Fr Francisco de Salamanca, which is protected by a magnificent plateresque grille. Here too, side by side on a sixteenth-century renaissance tomb, lie Don Gutiérrez de Monroy and Doña Constanza de Anaya, with grinning skulls as *mementi mori*. Painted vaults rise from gothic corbels, and a quaint *mudéjar* organ loft adds an exotic touch. The Madonna presents us with her little bald son who is worshipped by female saints, complete with the symbols by which they are identified, including Barbara with her tower, Lucy with her eyes and Catherine with her wheel. Jesus sits with his twelve apostles, flanked by a scene of his crucifixion and by two angels carrying a shield.

To my mind the Catedral Nueva is a magnificent oddity. In part the vagaries of its styles derive from the fact that money ran out before it was finished; in part they are due to quarrels among the canons, who were apt to replace architects abruptly; and in part they result from the fact that the cathedral took so long to build – from 1509 to 1733 – that late gothic, renaissance, plateresque and baroque architecture sit here side by side.

Inside, two aisles with side chapels flank a huge and lavishly decorated nave. Running around the cathedral are two balustrades: one, in the late gothic style with a frieze of animals and coats of arms, adorns the aisles and the ambulatory. Another, in the renaissance style, decorates the nave, which is further enhanced above and below the balustrade by medallions and portrait busts.

In the retrochoir are statues of St John the Baptist and the Madonna with her mother, St Anne, all sculpted by the mannerist Juan de Juni in the sixteenth century. They are matched in extravagance by the baroque eighteenth-century angels and the four doctors of the church, carved by Luis Salvador Carmona for the screen of the Capilla Mayor. Joaquín de Churriguera was responsible for designing the

---

This renaissance patio and staircase belong to the Fonseca College at Salamanca.

Above **The Torre del Gallo of Salamanca's Catedral Vieja, styled after the crossing of Zamora cathedral.**

Right **Evening sunshine picks out the jumbled architectural styles of Salamanca's Catedral Nueva.**

choir; it was begun in 1724 and finished by his brother Alberto some twenty years later. José de Lara sculpted the pews and Duperier made the screen.

Some of the side chapels are equally rich. Among the earliest are the first two in the north aisle, built by Juan Gil de Hontañón, and the first three in the south aisle by Juan de Alava. Of those by Alava, Archdeacon Francisco Sánchez de Palenzuela commissioned the second one in the south aisle, the Capilla Dorada, six years before his death in 1530. Also known as the Todos los Santos since it contains over a hundred statues of saints and a grisly *memento mori*, this chapel, protected by an imposing screen by Esteban de Buenamadre, is decorated with ceramics and contains the founder's tomb. In the next chapel is a copy of an Entombment of Jesus by Titian.

As you walk towards the ambulatory, hope that the Puerta del Patio Chico, on the south side, is open, for the finest view of the apses and lantern of the Catedral Vieja are to be had from the patio outside. Then visit the Relicario, above all for the sake of a celebrated relic of El Cid, a bronze Crucifix which accompanied him on his battles and was brought here by his chaplain Jerónimo Visquio, the first Bishop of Salamanca. Visquio himself lies further round the ambulatory, in a nineteenth-century tomb in the Capilla del Carmen which displays his own Crucifix, the eleventh-century 'Christ of the Battles'. On the way you pass the Capilla de los Dolores, with a Pietà by Luis Salvador Carmona.

It is high time to explore the exteriors of the two Salamanca cathedrals. Though the west façade of the Catedral Vieja was rebuilt in the nineteenth century, it incorporates a thirteenth-century carving of the Annunciation, done in the French gothic style. Walk around to the east end to see the triple semicircular apse and the superb octagonal lantern, the Torre del Gallo. Decorated with arcades and gables and reinforced by four turrets, it carries at its apex a cock, hence the name. This bizarre tower is not unique – it is matched for example by one at Zamora – but it is nonetheless decidedly unusual.

Juan Gil de Hontañón was the first architect of the new cathedral, and to him is owed the 110-metres-high tower (clad in protective masonry ever since the authorities took fright at the Lisbon earthquake of 1755). Rich sculpture ornaments the west façade, and over the main entrance are reliefs of the Magi and the shepherds of Bethlehem adoring the Infant Jesus. The north doorway is known as the Puerta de Ramos (the door of the branches) because its relief depicts Jesus entering Jerusalem on Palm Sunday. The *puerte* de Perdón, de San Clemente and de Obispo nearly match the Puerta de Ramos in gothic splendour.

The fifteenth-century works of Salamanca's finest painter, Fernando Gallego, are alone a sufficient reason for visiting the Diocesan Museum. But there are others: a prized possession is an organ which once belonged to a blind musician named Salinas, the subject of one of Luis de León's exquisite odes; the first room has a panelled ceiling which blends *mudéjar* with renaissance elements; and the masterpiece of the whole museum is a triptych of St Michael by Juan de Flandes.

The *calle* which runs from the Plaza Episcopal into Rivera del Puente is named Tentenecio, which means quiet, for here the patron saint of Salamanca, San Juan de Sahagún, calmed a mad bull which had careered away from its herd. After walking for a couple of minutes to the south of the old cathedral, you reach the Río Tormes and realize how ancient Salamanca really is, for the river is spanned here by a Roman bridge. Of the Puente Romano fifteen Roman arches still remain, while those at the far side of the river were rebuilt in 1677. Salamanca, which was captured by Hannibal in 217 BC, lies on the Roman road from Astorga to Merida. Vandals and Visigoths fought over the site until, in 711, it passed into the possession of the Moors, frequently changing hands in the long conflicts between them and the Christians. At the beginning of the twelfth century Alfonso of Castile encouraged Frenchmen to settle here, and during his reign Count Raymond of Burgundy (Don Raimundo de Borgoña),

---

An entertaining detail from the west portal of the Catedral Nueva, Salamanca.

Although these capitals in the cloister of the convent of Las Dueñas at Salamanca are plateresque in style, Rodrigo Gil de Hontañon has endowed them with much of the fantasy of the gothic.

who had helped him reconquer Salamanca, considerably enhanced the city. By the end of the century Salamanca's civic laws were famous.

The city began to decline only when, at the end of the sixteenth century, Felipe II set up a bishopric at Valladolid, removing that city, to which he had transferred his court, from the jurisdiction of the bishops of Salamanca. A further malign development was the expulsion of the Moors in 1610. Two wars – that of the Spanish Succession and that of the Liberation – brought havoc to Salamanca. The French were particularly brutal, destroying virtually the entire south-western part of the city in 1811. Even when the Duke of Wellington, commanding a combined Spanish and British force, defeated the French at Los Arapiles (4 kilometres to the south) on 22 July the following year, forcing the French to abandon Salamanca, the French

soldiers viciously plundered the city as they quitted it. It took half a century to recover.

By the river, on Calle Santiago, stands the twelfth-century church of Santiago, with its triple half-romanesque, half *mudéjar* apse, the sole reference to St James being a couple of cockle shells. From here Paseo del Rector Esperabe runs east to the Puerta San Pablo (of which hardly anything remains), where you turn left along Calle San Pablo to explore the quarter of ancient Salamanca that lies east of its cathedrals.

A right turn along Calle de San Buenaventura leads to two exquisite convents, the gothic convent of Las Dueñas on the left and the convent of San Esteban on the right. The first, founded in 1419, has a plateresque façade of 1533, sixteenth-century retables, baroque altars and plateresque cloisters. Even richer is the plateresque façade of the chapel of San Esteban, which was designed by Juan de Alava and built between 1524 and 1610. Covered in saints, with a frieze of men and animals, it has a central relief of the Stoning of St Stephen which was sculpted in 1610 by the Milanese Giovanni Antonio Ceroni. Among the assailants is a turbaned Moor, shown picking up a rock. Cardinal Juan de Alava, who paid for this chapel, had been a monk here, and his coat of arms appears on both sides of the arch. Inside is a single nave flanked by chapels, with three profusely decorated late seventeenth-century altars by José de Churriguera, who also made the huge reredos for the high altar in the 1690s. Salvador Carmona carved its animated statues of saints, but the gem of this piece is a twelfth-century statue of the Virgin Mary which came from the convent of La Vega (built outside the city walls in the mid twelfth century and long suppressed). Here too is another depiction of the Stoning of Stephen, this one painted in 1692 by Claudio Coello. José de Churriguera also carved the reredos of the chapel of Our Lady of the Rosary. The choir stalls, sculpted by Alfonso Balbás, seat 118 monks.

The stupendous façade of the convent chapel of San Esteban, Salamanca.

Ferdinand Alvarez de Toledo, Duke of Alva, lies here in a nineteenth-century tomb (though he died in 1582). So talented was this soldier and politician that he was a general by the age of 26 and commander-in-chief of the forces of Charles V by the time he was thirty. He so brilliantly defended Catalonia and Navarre that the emperor made him a duke, and he went on to defeat the Elector of Saxony at Mühlberg in 1547. In his attempt to destroy Protestantism after the revolt of the Netherlands, Alva's vicious and initially successful campaigns gradually turned sour (though the Pope presented him with a consecrated hat and sword as a defender of Catholicism). After the Dutch destroyed his fleet he returned to Spain, though he later set out again to conquer Portugal. Fittingly, in view of his career devoted to destroying Protestantism, on the wall above his tomb is a fresco of 1795 in which Antonio Palomino has depicted the triumph of the Catholic Church as a result of the work of the Dominicans. In the last chapel on the left is a sixteenth-century painting of the martyrdom of St Ursula.

The convent of San Esteban was founded by the Dominicans in the mid thirteenth century. Their conventual buildings lie to the south of the chapel, fronted by a splendid seventeenth-century renaissance portico covered in medallions and statues, with Doric and Ionic columns. Here in 1486, in the Salon de Profundis, Christopher Columbus managed to persuade his critics that his schemes were not insane. A statute of his ally, Fr Diego de Deza, stands by the entrance. The chapter-house and the royal cloister date from the sixteenth century, and the second, little, cloister was built in the fifteenth century.

East of San Esteban stands the honey-coloured Colegio de Calatrava, which was founded in 1552 and rebuilt in 1717 by Joaquín de Churriguera (with some later eighteenth-century modifications). Its pillars and porch are made of granite, as is the lower storey of the building. Beyond the college stands a church dedicated to the martyred Archbishop of Canterbury, Thomas Becket. Santo Tomás Cantuarense is romanesque, though its interior has been considerably altered, with churrigueresque and ceramic decoration

Built in 1175, only five years after the archbishop's assassination in Canterbury cathedral this is the first church ever to have been dedicated to Thomas Becket. Behind it, across Paseo de Canalejas, rises the Bernardine convent of Santa María de Jésus, with a sixteenth-century chapel built by Rodrigo Gil de Hontañón in 1552. A covered upper gallery runs around its huge patio as far as the choir of the church; inside are painted pendentives and a baroque tabernacle.

From the north-west corner of the convent of San Esteban, Calle de Juan de la Fuente runs to the tree-shaded Plaza de Colón, where a statue of Columbus, pointing westwards, was erected 400 years after his historic voyage to America. Busts of Isabella of Castile and Fr Diego de Deza are carved in relief on its plinth. Across the plaza rises the Palacio de Orellana and, in the north-west corner, the Casa de la Salina. Built in 1516 for the Fonseca family, the portico of its sumptuously decorated façade opens into a renaissance patio with a gallery on two sides. Sculpted corbels and grotesque figures support the gallery's upper storey.

In Calle Consuelo, on the north-east corner of the square, stands the Torre del Clavero. It was built in 1480 for Francisco de Sotomayor, who was 'clavero' (or custodian of the keys) of the knightly Order of Alcántara, which was founded in 1176 to defend Spain against the Moors and by now was immensely rich. The Torre is square at the base, becomes octagonal as it rises and ends up as a circular tower surrounded by eight turrets.

From here, skirting Plaza Mayor, walk past the covered market towards the church of San Julián. Up the steps ahead you can see the church of San Cristóbal, built in 1145, from whose parapet romanesque heads peep slyly down. Calle Bodegones leads to the sixteenth-century church of Sancti Spiritus; its plateresque south doorway by Berruguete is decorated with medallion busts of saints Peter and Paul and, in

On a corner of the Plaza de Colón rises the formidable fifteenth-century Torre del Clavero.

the pediment, St James the Great slaying Moors. Its finest chapel, dedicated to the Cristo de los Milagros ('Christ of the Miracles'), has a sixteenth-century panelled *mudéjar* ceiling. Here too is a twelfth-century Crucifixion and a retable from the studio of Gregorio Fernández.

Walk down Cuesta del Sancti-Spiritus and then turn right along the Gran Vía to reach the Plaza de la Constitución. Here stands the Torre del Aire, with its pretty gothic windows, all that remains of the fifteenth-century Fermoselle palace. Before making your way back to the Plaza Mayor, cross the little square and, from behind the palace opposite the Torre, take Calle Dean Paolo Benito and Calle de Vázquez Coronado to find the Plaza de San Boal. This is bordered by the Palacio del Marquéz de Almarza, where the Duke of Wellington chose to stay when he arrived in Madrid during the Peninsular War. Nearby rises the baroque church of Corpus Cristi which, as so often here, has a plateresque doorway. Due north is the romanesque church of San Marcos, which was built in 1202 and has three naves and three apses remarkably confined in a perfectly circular church. It also retains some fragmentary romanesque wall-paintings.

Calle de los Condos runs south from the Plaza de San Marcos to the house of Saint Teresa, once the cell of a convent where Teresa of Avila lived from 1570 to 1571. It has an unusually massive doorway for such a little house. Calle de Santa Teresa leads on to San Juan Bautista de Barbalos, a romanesque church with a fifteenth-century statue of the Virgin Mary and a churrigueresque retable.

From the Plaza Mayor, Calle del Prior runs west to Plazuela de Monterrey, in which stands a palace with two tall towers, conical chimneys and arrogant crests, built for the Monterrey family in the sixteenth century. Between 1598 and 1636 Gaspare de Acevedo y Zúñiga, Count of Monterrey and Viceroy of Naples, paid for the construction of the church and convent of Las Angustias Descalzas to the south of the palace. He intended the church, built by the Italian baroque architect Carlo Fontana, as his family mausoleum. Its glories are three paintings by José de Ribera, the first

of St Januarius and the second of the Madonna with St Dominic and St Anthony of Padua. The third, commonly reckoned Ribera's masterpiece, depicts the Immaculate Conception, with Mary gazing modestly to heaven, surrounded by angels. It enhances the chapel in which the Monterrey bones lie, beneath effigies of the count and his wife sculpted kneeling on their tomb by Giuliano Finelli.

In Spain St James the Great is never far away, and to the south-west along Calle de Ramón y Caja stands the sixteenth-century Colegio de Santiago Apostél, which once served as a seminary for Irish Catholics (it is also dubbed the Colegio de Nobles Irlandeses). Close by stands the hospice of 1760 in which they lodged, with its baroque doorway. A wall-plaque states that we are now a staggering 803.8 metres above sea level. The reredos of the college chapel, with carved figures and painted panels by Alonso de Berruguete, dates from 1529. The two-storey patio, designed by Diego de Siloé and built by Pedro de Ibarra, is an exquisite example of Spanish renaissance architecture. Above the plateresque doorway by Alonso de Covarrubias St James implacably slaughters Moors.

Archbishop Alonso de Fonseca founded this college, and the peaceful square in which it stands is called the Campo de Fonseca. To the north, across Calle de Ramón y Calal (the spelling varies from one street sign to another), is a wooded public garden and in the north-eastern corner of the *campo* is the exquisite chapel of Vera Cruz. Inside is an eighteenth-century Mater Dolorosa by Felipe de Corrál. This chapel was rebuilt in 1713 by Joaquín de Churriguera, but he preserved a sixteenth-century doorway.

Next to it rises the tall and elaborate convent of Las Ursulinas, in whose Capilla Mayor Archbishop Fonseca lies entombed, in a sepulchre designed by Diego de Siloé. An unexpected treat in the convent's museum is a triptych by Michelangelo reproducing the Descent from the Cross which he painted for the Sistine Chapel

---

Late gothic vaults soar above the chapel of the Fonseca College.

in Rome. And on the south side of Las Ursulinas stands the mid sixteenth-century House of the Dead (the Casa de las Muertes), so called because its rich plateresque façade incorporates skulls as well as busts of the Fonseca family; it is said to be by Diego de Siloé.

Beside it stands a house once occupied by Miguel de Unamuno. A remarkable philosopher and poet, born at Bilbao in 1864, he became professor of Greek at Salamanca in 1892. Forced into exile as a republican from 1924 to 1930, he was reinstated in 1931 and became rector of the university.

This Spanish patriot responded passionately to his cultural heritage. He wrote a long poetical meditation on a Crucifixion by Velázquez which hangs in the Prado, devoting entire stanzas to the limbs and posture of the dead Saviour:

> *You bow your head upon your breast*
> *just as a lily withered by the sun*
> *bends over its stalk...*
> *Your face is hidden,*
> *as out of shame for the human race.*

Unamuno believed in virility, almost as part of faith. 'We must husband virility to beget sons of the spirit', he wrote in *The Agony of Christianity*, adding that as well as faith and the will to believe he held that men and women possessed 'a lust for belief, the appetite for belief'. In his best-known work, *Del sentimiento trágico de la vida* (*The Tragic Sense of Life*), he admitted to being a heretic since he refused to accept the easy comforts of Catholicism, agnosticism or rationalism. And he asked his readers to consider how it had come about that among the words that English has borrowed from Spanish, such as *siesta*, *camarilla* and *guerilla*, should be found the word *desperado*. 'It is despair, and

A tower and remains of the walls of Madrigal de las Altas Torres.

despair alone', he declared, 'that engenders heroic hope, absurd hope, insane hope.'

In the square outside his home in Salamanca is a modern bronze statue of Unamuno. His cloak swirls around him and his beard juts forward; an authentic Spanish *desperado*.

Nineteen kilometres through the wooded hills south-east of Salamanca is a town renowned for its connection with St Teresa of Avila. Alba de Tormes is dominated by its sixteenth-century keep high up above the town, all that remains of the castle of the dukes of Alba, which was almost entirely destroyed in 1819 during the War of Independence. The town itself lies beside the Río Tormes, with its 22-arched medieval bridge. A bronze larger-than life statue of the saint stands outside her disappointingly modern basilica, next to the Carmelite convent which she founded in 1471; it was here that she died in 1582 and her relics are now preserved by the main altar. The convent has a

Castillo de Buen Amor, some 25 kilometres north of Salamanca, was founded as a fortress by Alfonso de León in 1227 and later refitted as a country residence for Ferdinand and Isabella.

151

Single-storey houses rise above the arcades of the Plaza de la Villa at Arévalo.

renaissance-baroque doorway depicting the Angel Gabriel appearing to the Virgin Mary.

Beside some of the exquisite spots in this region of Castile, Alba de Tormes seems a nonedescript town, yet it boasts two fine twelfth-century churches in San Juan and Santiago (with a delightful row of saints on the brick façade of the latter), as well as San Miguel which is only a hundred years younger – all three of them built in the *mudéjar*-romanesque style. San Juan also has a fourteenth-century statue of Jesus and a churrigueresque reredos sculpted in 1771, while the reredos of Santiago dates from the sixteenth century.

The Tormes is but one of the rivers of this region that are stocked with trout, tench, barbel and carp, while the Aldeadávila is a fertile source of crayfish. Small wonder that at Salamanca a *sopa de pescado* is crammed with huge chunks of white fish, pieces of crab and a mass of other shellfish. In my view it goes well with an unpretentious Vino de Mesa Blanco,

bottled by Carbajosa de la Sagrada, which is usually mellow and nearly as yellow as the fish soup. Fish is not the only delicacy of this region (though grilled *merluza* and *languado* are other local favourites), and in the restaurants diners can be seen tucking into *pisto* – a hot ratatouille on top of which are chopped up hard-boiled eggs – or else roast veal in a piquant sauce.

Leaving Alba de Tormes for Peñaranda de Bracamonte, which lies 28 kilometres to the north-east, you pass the convent of Santa Isabel, which was built in 1481, and the convent of las Benitas, which was rebuilt in 1734, retaining its sixteenth-century portal. Though semi-industrialized, the little town of Peñaranda de Bracamonte has a sixteenth-century church built in a transitional style between gothic and renaissance, and a fifteenth-century palace. Here too stands a Carmelite convent founded by the Count of Peñaranda in the seventeenth century. Inside the convent chapel are paintings by Lucas Jordán and Andrea Vaccaro.

Another 28 kilometres north-east stands a remote village with an even more romantic-sounding name than Peñaranda de Bracamonte. Madrigal de las Altas Torres is surrounded by twelfth- and thirteenth-century walls, a few of whose towers have survived the centuries. This was the birthplace of Isabella the Catholic, the resolute partner of Ferdinand of Aragon, and the convent of the Madres Angustinas incorporates part of the palace where she was born. She was baptized in its chapel, which has a *mudéjar* ceiling – ironically in view of the fact that it was she and her husband who ended centuries of toleration of the Moors who created such gems.

Drive east from Madrigal de las Altas Torres to Arévalo, in whose fourteenth-century castle the future queen spent part of her childhood; she also lived at one time in the convent of San Bernardo el Real. In the Plaza de la Villa rise two *mudéjar* brick towers belonging to the church of San Martín. The square itself is surrounded by humble houses with balconies

Dusk falls over the gothic-*mudéjar* castle at Coca.

supported by stone or wooden pillars, but elsewhere in the narrow streets of Arévalo are more substantial sixteenth-century seigneurial houses. The church of San Miguel has a fine baroque reredos; that in the chapel of Alonso de Avila Monroy in San Salvador was begun by Juan de Juni in 1577 and finished by his son.

Drive north-east from Arévalo, crossing the N403 at San Cristóbal de la Vega and continuing through pines to the enchanting town of Coca. Its astonishing, delicately coloured brick castle blends gothic and *mudéjar* building techniques into a work of high art. Archbishop Alonso de Fonseca commissioned the building in the fifteenth century, and the craftsmen he employed created for him a large square fortress with a double, crenellated ring wall, encorbelled turrets and a deep, walled moat. The dukes of Fonseca lie today in renaissance tombs inside the fifteenth-century parish church of Santa María la Mayor.

Olmedo lies north-west of Coca, and derives its name from the elm trees which first sheltered the nascent town. Some walls remain from the once powerful fortress. Among its brick *mudéjar* churches, San Miguel has several baroque reredoses, while the thirteenth-century San Andrés has one carved by Berruguete in 1526.

Beyond Olmedo is Medina del Campo, which has superb churches dating from the late Middle Ages and the Renaissance, when it was at the height of its prosperity. Sheep brought wealth to this city, and even today its sheep fairs are the most important in Spain. As you approach the town you pass the thirteenth- and fifteenth-century Castillo de la Mota, a brick castle set on a ridge, with a massive keep surrounded by crenellated walls. Inside the town the gothic style is exemplified in the Plaza Mayor by the early sixteenth-century church of San Antolín, behind whose high altar is a plateresque reredos. And the Renaissance is represented by the façade and re-strained inner patio of the Palacio de Dueñas, built for a rich banker of the town named Rodrigo de Dueñas, and by another façade, which once fronted the royal palace of Medina del Campo, in the Plaza Mayor. It was here in 1504 that Isabella of Castile died. As for the other buildings of the plaza, the finest is the eighteenth-century Casa Consistoriales, the administrative centre of the town.

To the west is Nava del Rey, where the church of Los Santos Juanes has a sacristy built by Alberto de Churriguera and an early seventeenth-century reredos by Gregorio Fernández. At Alaéjos turn left along the N620 to drive back to Salamanca, and continue on the same road to Ciudad Rodrigo. Delightfully situated on a hill beside the Río Agueda, the town is still protected by 2 kilometres of twelfth-century walls. On this same site the Celts established a fortified camp, which the Romans took over and reinforced. Then the Moors transformed the camp into an *alcázar*, which was taken from them in the eleventh century by the man after whom the city is named, Rodrigo González Girón. The castle was reconstructed in the fourteenth century, and is now a National Parador.

For the most part the walls of Ciudad Rodrigo enclose a renaissance city. In the Plaza Mayor two round towers flank the sixteenth-century arcaded Ayuntamiento, which is complemented in the same square by the renaissance Palacio de Cueto. The powerful doors of this palace, the larger one embraced by a polylobed stone arch, seem designed to deter visitors, but in the upper storeys this sternness melts away. It is replaced by the delicacy of a plateresque frieze running between two rows of wrought iron balconies charmingly sculpted with medallions; coats of arms decorate the corners of the building and the whole is topped by a renaissance balustrade.

Another plateresque façade, with twisting columns, enlivens the fifteenth-century Palacio de los Castros, which stretches alongside Plaza del Conde. Two carved lions glare down at you as you pass through the porch to view its patio. Artesonado ceilings embellish the sixteenth-century Casa de los Vazques nearby, while in the late sixteenth-century Herreran Capilla de Cerralbo, on the Plazuela del Buen Alcalde, is a reredos

---

In the Plaza Mayor at Ciudad Rodrigo this plateresque frieze graces the façade of the Palacio de Cueto.

6
From Avila to Segovia
Avila – El Escorial – Segovia

No city in Spain has finer medieval walls than tiny Avila. To arrive there after dark, when the walls are softly illuminated, is a thrilling experience. They tower massively above you as you drive around them. Built in the last decade of the eleventh century, and stretching for some $2\frac{1}{2}$ kilometres, these dark granite crenellated walls enclose the ancient city in a powerful stone rectangle, 12 metres high and 3 metres thick, buttressed, every 25 metres or so, by 86 towers. Nine gates, all of them monumental and defended by sturdy turrets, pierce the walls. Two, the Puerta del Alcázar and the Puerta de San Vicente at the north-east corner of the city, are outstanding. Others, such as the venerable and doddery gate known as Madrigal de las Altas Torres, seem almost to have forgotten why they are here.

The situation of Avila, on a flat-topped ridge with three precipitous sides (it is the highest city in Spain), made it almost impregnable even before the walls were built. To the west of the city flows the River Adaja, beyond which rise the Paramera de Avila and the Sierra de Avila, while to the east, as a further protection, rises the Sierra de Malagón. The Romans set up a military base on the site (Roman remains were later incorporated in the medieval walls) and, as elsewhere in Castile, the Moors and the Christians battled for centuries to control the city. The Christians triumphed only under Alfonso VI. Not so magnanimous as elsewhere in Castile, Alfonso's successors unwisely expelled both the Jews and the Moors, actions which inevitably led to the economic and cultural decline of the city.

Yet Avila remains spectacular. The city retains some seigneurial dwellings of outstanding beauty, from thirteenth-century palaces to noble sixteenth-century houses. Close by the Puerta de San Vicente, whose twin circular towers guard a bridge-like parapet, is the finest romanesque building in Avila, the sandstone church of San Vicente, which actually lies outside the walls, on the spot where its patron was martyred in the fourth century. Begun in the twelfth century, the church was finished only in the fifteenth. The thirteenth-century romanesque double doorway in the west front is embellished with contemporary terra-cotta statues, still impressive though mutilated, the apostles carved in a fashion which derives from the Burgundian masters. Two towers rise on either side of the west façade: the north tower dates from the twelfth to the fifteenth century, while the south tower was restored in the nineteenth century; still unfinished, it looks squat and depressed, as if longing finally to be given its four-sided pointed cap.

Delay the pleasure of seeing the breathtaking interior of this church by walking around the south side,

Left The massive medieval walls and towers which encircle Avila.

Above Beyond the Almarza family palace at Avila rises the tower of the Guzmán palace.

163

where a granite cloister protects the twelfth-century statues of the south entrance. A galaxy of quaint romanesque creatures peers down from its parapet. The statues over the porch represent St Vincent, his sister St Sabina, and the visit of the Angel Gabriel to the Virgin Mary.

Inside, the nave of the church is entirely romanesque, and the transepts, choir and three painted, semicircular apses gracefully hint at the Gothic. Behind the main altar rises a huge baroque eighteenth-century reredos by Bartolomé Carducho. The patron saint of the church, the early fourth-century martyr St Vincent, lies, along with his martyred sisters St Sabina and St Cristeta, underneath the lantern of the church in a superb thirteenth-century sarcophagus. Decorated with reliefs, the finest of which depicts the Adoration of the Magi, the sarcophagus is covered by a gothic canopy of 1465.

The three saints were martyred on the rock on which this church was built, and you can still see the fateful spot in the crypt where their tomb now lies. In case anyone might imagine martyrdom to be a pleasant experience, their sarcophagus savagely depicts their tortures, showing their bodies being cruelly stripped and crushed to death while their souls ascend to heaven. The crypt is worth visiting simply to see two statues of the Virgin Mary, one twelfth-century romanesque, the other fifteenth-century gothic. And to the east of the tomb of the saints hangs a fourteenth-century painting of Christ crucified, flanked by his mother and St John.

Still outside the walls, the church of San Andrés, to the north of San Vicente, is another twelfth- and thirteenth-century romanesque building. But the most impressive walk from San Vicente is south along Calle de San Segundo, past a formal garden and on beside the city walls. Turn left where the fortified apse of Avila cathedral bursts through the walls, and in the triangular Plazuela de Nalvillos you will find the renais-

A renaissance carving set in the romanesque south porch of San Vicente.

sance deanery (or Casa de los Deanes) which now serves as the city museum. It houses Celtic-Iberian finds, romanesque, gothic and renaissance statues, a triptych attributed to Hans Memling and eighteenth-century Brussels tapestries. Close by is the sculpted south doorway of the romanesque church of Santo Tomé el Viejo, which is now a museum of gravestones. From here, Calle de Estrada runs on beside a renaissance palace to a plaza dedicated to Avila's most celebrated daughter, St Teresa, at the centre of which rises a white column crowned with her statue.

This outstanding woman was born in 1509, daughter of the 17-year-old Beatriz de Ahumada. She was 7 when she and her brother Rodrigo decided to die as martyrs, secretly quitting their home with the intention of being beheaded by the Moors. Fortunately an uncle discovered them leaving Avila by the city's Roman bridge and took them back to their parents. This impetuous piety soon disappeared as Teresa

The belfry of the church of San Vicente. Note the figures hiding in the niches of the gutter.

165

developed into an exceedingly beautiful young wo-man. She set her heart on marrying one of her handsome cousins, but her father would have none of it. When she was only 15 her mother died, leaving Teresa's father to cope with ten children. The young girl might now have proved her ability to sew and run a household, but her mother's death had left her deeply disturbed and she appealed to the Blessed Virgin Mary for succour. Her father made a crucial decision to entrust her to the care of the Augustinian nuns of Santa María de Gracia. As Teresa's self-composure returned, so did her piety. On her return home, her father was disconcerted by her announce-ment that she intended to become a nun. When he opposed the plan she ran away, and on 2 November 1535 she entered the Carmelite monastery of the Encarnación at Avila. Her father gave in and in 1536 Teresa received the habit.

Yet, as her autobiography reveals, she was as yet still an egoistic creature, longing for human praise. She fell seriously ill, remaining an invalid for eighteen years and once sinking into a coma which lasted for four days and led many to believe she had died. Then at the age of 39, as she meditated before an image of the wounded Jesus, her vanity disappeared. Thenceforth Teresa experienced within her heart the constant presence of God. Her newly found rapture and her refusal to adopt a vigorously ascetic life annoyed many of her fellow Christians, including some of her confes-sors and superiors, who insisted that Teresa's visions and divine happiness were the work of the devil, but she was greatly encouraged by St Peter of Alcántara, who told her to persist in her ways, adding that 'we all suffer such trials'.

Peter also encouraged her plan to found a new convent at Avila which would base itself on the ancient tradition established by the nuns of Mount Carmel, and he espoused her cause in Rome. In spite of continual opposition, the convent was founded, sprouting daughter houses at Malagon, Valladolid,

Stormy dawn light over the Plaza de Santa Teresa.

This modern statue of St Teresa rests outside the walls of Avila.

Toledo, Pastrana, Salamanca and Alba de Tormes. She enlisted the aid of her great contemporary St John of the Cross, who agreed to be confessor to her nuns. Writing brilliant mystical treatises, Teresa continued to found new convents, the last four at Palencia and Soria (in 1581) and at Burgos and Granada (in 1582). She died in the year of her two last foundations, to be buried at Alba. By this time her writings, particularly *The Way of Perfection* and *The Interior Castle*, together with those of St John of the Cross, had created an extraordinary spiritual awakening in Spanish Catholi-cism and beyond it.

Pope Paul V beatified her forty years after her death. Without waiting for her canonization, in 1617 the Spanish parliament declared her patroness of Spain, at which the satirist Quevedo wrote a mordant pamphlet declaring that his country had exchanged a warrior patron for a woman. He was wrong, for Santiago Matamoros remains co-patron of the country. At Avila the major festival, apart from that of Holy Week, takes place from 8 October to 15 October, when the citizens dance in the streets and organize contests in honour of Teresa. A less than spiritual legacy of 'La Santa', as she is known, is a sugary sweetmeat known as *Yemas de Santa Teresa*, promoted in every confectioner's shop in Avila. As for the less sickly gastronomic delicacies of the city, whereas normally in Castile *trucha a la navarra* indicates that the trout has been marinaded in wine and herbs, here I have had it wrapped in really crispy bacon, which is delicious. The *sopa de pescado* in Avila is also quite different from that in, say, Salamanca, for here it is enriched with squid and bits of rice. Washed down with a white Vino Cebreros, any meal tastes better, though the alcohol content of this wine makes it advisable to indulge only in the evening.

At the easternmost end of the Plaza de Santa Teresa stands the church of San Pedro, yet another superb romanesque church, built of sandstone, with a twelfth-century romanesque nave. Its west façade is pierced by a rose window that looks like a sturdy wagon wheel, and the doorway is a wide and perfectly round arch. The transepts, choir, lantern and triple nave are transitional gothic in style, and the main retable is churrigueresque. The north aisle is a little gallery of fine art, with a tiny plateresque retable of 1536 which bears an Italian statue of the Madonna, paintings of the school of Pedro Berruguete and a late seventeenth-century statue of St Peter in chains by Morán.

Across the Plaza de Santa Teresa is Avila's second finest gateway, the Puerta del Alcázar, which dwarfs every passer-by. The Catholic Kings have stamped their escutcheon on either side. Just to the south of San Pedro stands the church of Santa María la Antigua. And some ten minutes away, to the south-east and up a picturesque climb, stands the Dominican convent of Santo Tomás. Though ostensibly dedicated to St Thomas Aquinas, it was founded by the first Inquisitor-General, Tomás de Torquemada, in 1482. The convent became a favourite resting place of the Catholic Kings, and one of its three cloisters is dubbed the Claustro de los Reyes. Their arms also decorate the portal of the late gothic convent church, whose basic

architectural style is concealed by its four-storey classical façade. The chief treasure of this church is a painted fifteenth-century retable on the high altar, probably by Pedro Berruguette. It depicts St Thomas Aquinas, the greatest of all Dominican philosophers and theologians, surrounded by angels. On either side are scenes from his life, while the glory of St Thomas is attested by the presence in the painting of fellow saints Lawrence, Augustine, John, Matthew, Jerome and Sebastian.

The church's second greatest treasure is a renaissance monument sculpted by the Florentine Domenico Fancelli to commemorate and house the mortal remains of the only son of Ferdinand and Isabella, Juan, who died in 1497 aged 19. He lies on his ornamented sarcophagus, his hands on his sword. Fancelli also carved the tomb of Hernán Nuñes de Arnalte, and that of the prince's governess, Juana de Velázquez de la Torre, which stands in the third chapel on the north side of the church. The late gothic choir stalls are, as one would expect, emblazoned with the coat of arms of Ferdinand and Isabella, and are the work of Martín Sánchez.

From the south-east corner of the city walls, the Paseo del Rastro runs west as far as the Puerta de Santa Teresa, offering splendid views of the Amblés valley and the mountains. Below can be seen first the convent of Nuestra Señora de Gracia, where St Teresa of Avila went as a schoolgirl, and then the romanesque-ogival church of Santiago. Its fourteenth-century cylindrical tower culminates in a needle-sharp sixteenth-century spire; the doorway is renaissance and the retable of the high altar dates from the early eighteenth century.

Through the Puerta de Santa Teresa stands the Herreran church built in 1636 on the site of the house where Teresa was born in 1515. She appears in ecstasy over the doorway of the façade, and inside she is depicted in the classical reredos over the high altar, while her relics lie in the chapel of Santa Teresa,

A quiet cloister of the convent of Santo Tomás.

This wild man guards the main entrance to Avila cathedral.

which stands on the very site of her home. Here the reredos is baroque.

This church is flanked by the mid sixteenth-century Palacio de los Núñez Vela (now the Palace of Justice) and the Torreón de los Guzmanes, in the Plaza del General Mola to the right. The powerful crenellated tower in this square rises from the Casa del Conde de Oñato, which looks across at the classical façade of the Casa de Superunda. Here too is a bronze, set up in 1962, of that other great Avilan saint, John of the Cross. From this square you can see the romanesque-gothic Palacio de los Dávila in Plaza del Rastro. It stretches as far as the Plaza de Pedro Dávila, where its façade is even mightier, with a couple of heralds on prancing steeds sculpted over the main doorway and two hairy men kneeling beside the family coat of arms. I do not know why the Dávila motto, inscribed around this scene, should be (in translation), 'When one door opens, another closes.'

A sign here points towards the church of San Juan and the Plaza de la Victoria, a partly arcaded square which takes its name from the greatest Spanish polyphonic composer, Tomás Luis de Victoria. On one side rises the balconied Ayuntamiento, on the other the church of San Juan, with its brick belfry and simple romanesque doorway.

Calle de los Reyes Católicos runs east from here, past the romanesque convent of Nuestra Señora de las Nieves to Avila's cathedral. The building, with its mighty north tower, shapes up to you like a prize-fighter. A closer look reveals a gentler aspect, however, ogival arches betraying the transition from romanesque to gothic. Dedicated to San Salvador, the cathedral is said to have been founded by Fernán González, Count of Castile, who died in 970. The building we see today was begun 120 years later, and the mighty, semicircular east end, whose battlements push out beyond the walls of Avila, dates from this foundation. It represents a major change in Spanish architecture – the influence of the French – for the architect who began work on it around the mid twelfth century was a Burgundian whom we know as Maître Fruchel. As well as creating a house of God, he was building an integral part of the defences of Avila; from this east end a passage communicates with the shielded raised path which runs along the top of the city walls.

Even the west end of the cathedral is well protected. Two fifteenth-century gothic towers (one unfinished and later redone in the baroque style) were built for the main façade by Juan de Guas, and a couple of sculpted lions and two wild mace-bearers, carved in granite, menace you as you walk up to admire the sixteenth-century sculptures on the main entrance. Inside, the nave is remarkably small, but its height more than compensates for this. On the left as you enter is a fourteenth-century gothic font. By contrast with the nave, the aisles are low and wide. Here is another double ambulatory, a notion borrowed from France and employed here not only as a result of the influence of French architects but also because of the demands of pilgrims, who would process around the ambulatories in orderly fashion, worshipping before the altars of the nine exquisite chapels and prostrating themselves before venerated relics. Flowers and complex tracery betray the hands of fourteenth-century master masons. The colours of the granite in the little transept are gorgeous.

The choir occupies the centre of the cathedral, a church within a church. As you walk around it you will see two scenes of holy slaughter: St George slaying the dragon which is threatening a maiden, while below him St Matthew ponders his gospel; and a gruesome Santiago Matamoros, underneath whom is St John the Evangelist, identified by his eagle.

The decoration becomes more flamboyant and also less belligerent in the renaissance tomb, possibly by Domenico Fancelli, of Bishop Alfonso Tostado de Madrigal, who died in 1455. His sculpted effigy, the work of Vasco de la Zarza, sits at a writing desk in a marvellously ornate alabaster cope. Above him the shepherds and the Magi herald the birth of his Saviour, watched over by God the Father. Flanking the bishop are the four evangelists and below him the symbols of the seven heavenly virtues. Among the details of this monument, Adam and Eve shamefully cover their private parts, St Hubertus protects a beleaguered stag from the hunters and St Jerome broods beside his lion, which carries a bell on its paw. Nearby are St Martin of Tours, and St Mark – whose bull has a bell on its horn. As for Bishop Alfonso, his much simpler fifteeenth-century tomb contrasts with this elaborate yet successful monument.

As in almost all great Spanish cathedrals, the choir stalls are lovely; these are the work of a Dutchman named Cornelis who worked here from 1536 to 1547. Two pulpits, one plateresque, the other delicate and renaissance in style, separate the choir from the Capilla Mayor, which is protected by two plateresque grilles. In the reredos of the high altar in the Capilla Mayor, Avila has once again been blessed with a masterpiece. It is by Pedro Berruguete, Juan de Borgõna and Santa Cruz, and it includes depictions of ten episodes from the life of Christ, and portraits of saints Peter, Paul, James, Simon, Andrew and Jude, and of the four doctors of the church and the four evangelists. This retable has afforded art historians considerable entertainment, for it is far from easy to distinguish one hand from another. Finally, the art of the renaissance makes its appearance in Avila cathedral in the altars on either side of the Capilla Mayor.

The trascoro is decorated with reliefs of scenes from the early life of Christ, carved around 1530. Among some homely touches are the pigeons on the roof of the cattle shed in which Jesus was born and a pair of scissors his mother has left on a cushion. Of the three Magi, the Negro king is accompanied by a little black servant. Both Mary and Joseph are depicted in identical fashion in each scene, Joseph particularly fetching with his stick, bald head (with a few remaining tufts of hair) and beard, and Mary with her hair exquisitely curled throughout, even in the Flight into Egypt. Savagery returns with the Slaughter of the Innocents, the soldiers' faces suitably ugly, while the compassionate, even sad face of God the Father surveys the whole complex relief.

These are not the only treasures of Avila cathedral. A romanesque doorway with a fine plateresque grille leads to the gothic cloisters, which were built in the fourteenth century. And in the vestry is an alabaster Flagellation of 1553; the baroque vestment chests carry mirrors to enable the clergy to make sure that they are well turned out before they appear before the laity. Connecting the vestry with the sacristy is a gothic chapel which has been turned into a little religious museum, with a plateresque screen and a huge silver-gilt altar and reredos. Displayed here are fascinating fifteenth-century psalters, with annotated music, as well as a twelfth-century romanesque Crucifix. The altar of the gothic sacristy itself may be the work of Pedro Berruguete. And in the vestibule is a famous silver-gilt monstrance made by Juan de Arfe in 1571. In the middle of the monstrance is a deliciously executed scene: while Abraham prepares to sacrifice his son Isaac, an angel descends to prevent him and a ram caught in a thicket waits helplessly to be sacrificed instead.

We have not yet explored the city north of its walls. To reach this quarter from the cathedral, take the Calle del Tostado, and on a corner of the cathedral square you will find the Casa del Marqués de Velada. Charles V enjoyed its three-storey patio when he stayed here on a visit to Avila. Turn left along the Calle de Lopez Nuñes and you will pass by the Casa de los Verdugo y los Aguilas before reaching the funeral chapel of Mosén Rubí de Bracamonte, now a Dominican convent, which was built in the gothic and renaissance styles at the beginning of the sixteenth century. It houses the sepulchre of its founder, Doña María de Herrera, who placed the chapel under the protection of the French-Jewish Bracamonte family.

North of here are the Fuente del Sol (the fountain of the sun) and the Puerta del Sol, from which a tree-lined walk takes us to the chapel of San Martín, whose rebuilding in 1706 sensitively retained its romanesque tower. To the left, along another tree-shaded route, is the romanesque-*mudéjar* cemetery chapel of Santa María de la Cabeza, who was the sister of St Ildefonso.

Directly north is a spot sanctified by Teresa of Avila. Founded in 1499, the convent of the Encarnación was taken over by Carmelite nuns in 1515. Eighteen years later St Teresa took her vows, and she stayed here for the next 27 years. Some of her remains, as well as her manuscripts, are preserved in the cloister. Alas, the church of Santa María della Vittoria in Rome has the notorious statue which Bernini sculpted of St Teresa in ecstasy, and the convent of the Encarnación in Avila has to make do with a copy.

Compared with Teresa, the first Bishop of Avila, St Secondo, is easily forgotten, so it becomes an act of historical piety to walk west from her convent to the little romanesque hermitage of San Segundo. The visit is worth the trouble, even if the hermitage is closed. This is early twelfth-century romanesque at its most rustic, a simple belfry and a pretty doorway enhancing a humble house of God virtually hidden among the trees, with chickens and hens scuttling about outside.

If the hermitage is open a visit becomes a delightful experience. Bishop Secondo lies inside, in a rather more flamboyant alabaster tomb than I fear he would have liked; it is the work of Juan de Juni and dates from 1573. A little hole below it allows the visitor to peer down at his relics. On a reredos to the right he is depicted in a scarlet cope and mitre, with a carved figure of St Teresa above him. In the same chapel is a statue of the saint who can cure toothache, Apollonia.

Romanesque sirens and a lion with its prey in its jaws are sculpted on a capital. The frescoed apse, which is off-centre, has a magnificent baroque reredos, which depicts the doctors of the church, including St Augustine as a black man (which, though rarely represented as such, he almost certainly was). The central sculpture of this reredos is a vicious Santiago Matamoros, while the medicinal work of St Apollonia is complemented by that of St Lucy (who cures failing eyesight) and St Agatha (who specializes in heart disease). Another altar-piece, dedicated to St Blas, carries a renaissance Annunciation, and two granite pillars bear twin sets of little romanesque stoups, two of them with locked covers, presumably to stop witches stealing holy water for their own nefarious purposes.

St Secondo's hermitage stands outside the north-west corner of the walls which protect Avila; but hermits have never relied for their protection on earthly fortifications.

The countryside around the city has an austere grandeur, with hills rising to some 1500 metres above sea level and, in the background, hostile, snow-capped mountains. Leaving Avila, the C505 skirts the noble landscape of the Campo Azálvaro, crossing the Valde-lavia ridge and running eastwards towards El Escorial. It climbs high into the Sierra de Gredos, a pine-decked range whose granite rocks, beloved of mountaineers, are the home of wild, curly-horned goats; the highest peak, Moro Almanzor, reaches 2607 metres. The road passes Las Navas del Marqués, where in the sixteenth century the dukes of Medinaceli built themselves a castle with a beautiful renaissance patio. Then it twists downhill, and there below, in a spectacular setting at the foot of the Sierra de Guadarrama, stands the palace, pantheon and monastery of San Lorenzo de El Escorial.

King Felipe II commissioned it to commemorate his

The church of Chatmartin, west of Avila.

victory over the French at Saint Quentin on St Lawrence's day, 10 August 1557, and the building mimics in its plan the gridiron on which the saint was martyred. Felipe's first architect was Juan Bautista de Toledo, and after his death in 1567 the work was continued by Juan de Herrera, who completed it in 1584. I wonder whether the king expected his monks to die of cold, for in winter the spot is invariably freezing. True, its climate in summer is preferable to the fetid heat of Madrid, but in the end Felipe chose not to work at El Escorial. He did, however, die here, in a humble bed which can still be seen in the palace.

Huge and gaunt, the cold granite mass of El Escorial is as forbidding as the winter weather, and even its box parterres remain equally formal. The building seems to mirror the melancholy of the last years of the monarch who built it. In his youth the prince had responded warmly to the renaissance, spending 1548 to 1551 on a tour of Italy, Germany and the Low Countries and developing a taste for contemporary foreign artists (among the thousand paintings he gave to El Escorial were thirty canvases by Titian and twenty by Hieronymus Bosch). But as the troubles of his long reign began to overwhelm him, the five times widowed king withdrew into himself. The successive portraits you see on the walls of El Escorial reveal his increasing gloom, his black garb scarcely relieved by the tiny gold insignia of the Golden Fleece.

The Patio de los Evangelistas, the monastery cloister of San Lorenzo de El Escorial, is frescoed with the history of redemption by the sixteenth-century Italian Pellegrino Tibaldi, a series beginning with the birth of the Virgin Mary and ending with the Last Judgment. But most of the decoration of the monastery is devoted to the glorification of the royal house of Spain, on whose lands, as Felipe once boasted, the sun would never set. Lucas Jordán frescoed the ceiling of the staircase which rises from this cloister with a scene entitled *The Glorification of the Spanish Monarchy*.

As aloof, cold and impressive as the sovereign for which it was built: El Escorial.

A sternly elegant patio leading into the gardens of El Escorial.

The Palacio Real incorporates the Sala de Batallas, a long gallery lined with battle scenes, and a museum housing much of the king's magnificent art collection. Among the first works you encounter are a remarkably foreshortened Adoration of the Shepherds by Tintoretto, an almost three-dimensional Crucifixion by Roger van der Weyden, and two paintings by Fernandez Navarette, known as El Mudo because he was dumb: the first depicts the beheading of St James the Great; the second St Jerome (on whose book is painted '1569 I. F. MUDO IO FECIT'). Other notable works, in particular José de Ribera's portrait of Aesop and Zurbarán's St Peter of Alcántara, hang nearby. Then, in the portrait room of the royal palace, are the Habsburgs, all with their prominent chins. Incidental treats are the inlaid doors of these rooms.

From here you descend to the creepy Panteón de los Reyes, the mausoleum of the kings, their corpses lying on shelves around an octagonal chapel decorated in gilded bronze and red and grey marble. Here too are the bodies of the queens of Spain, but only of those who gave birth to a future king. The tomb of the Emperor Charles V is inscribed CAROLVS V OMP. ET. REY. Three tombs still await future royal bodies.

Next comes the Panteón de los Infantes, housing the tombs of princes and princesses who never reached the throne, roomful after roomful. Felipe's illegitimate half-brother, Don Juan of Austria, lies in a room of his own, his recumbent effigy holding his sword. On one side is inscribed INMORTALIS EST ENIM MEMORIA ILLVS ('His memory is immortal'). On the other, with breathtakingly arrogant blasphemy, are the words used by the fourth gospel of St John the Baptist: FVIT HOMO MISSVS A DEO CVI NOMEN ERAT JOANNES ('There was a man sent from God whose name was John'). Along with these princes and princesses lie lots of royal children, in a tomb like a giant wedding cake.

It is a relief to climb from this grim spot to the delightfully decorated Salas Capitulares (or Chapterhouses). Here hang Titian's St Jerome and four El Grecos. In the next room are more Titians and some huge and magnificent works by Veronese. The last room houses nine works by Hieronymus Bosch; they include his *Way to Calvary*, which is set against a Flemish background, and a triptych illustrating the seven deadly sins between scenes of heaven and hell. In his *Creation* the beasts happily disport themselves, a monkey riding on a lion's back.

The façade of the basilica of El Escorial is adorned with the statues of six Old Testament kings, Jehosephat, Hezekiah, David, Solomon, Josiah and Manasseh, all carved by Juan Bautista Monegro, as was the statue of St Lawrence over the main entrance to El Escorial. The massive building is crowned with a dome typical of the work of Juan de Herrera. And inside this frowning basilica are the sculpted figures of the royal family, worshipping on either side of the high altar. Herrera designed the huge reredos, between whose jasper columns are eight paintings by Italian artists and fifteen statues from the workshop of Pompeo Leoni. Another Italian masterpiece is the marble Crucifixion by Benvenuto Cellini in one of the chapels.

Only the library, it seems to me, is built on a human scale, and among the fine illustrated manuscripts on display are some in Arabic (1886 of them to be exact, compared with 2086 in Latin and 582 in Greek).

Felipe requisitioned land around the monastery to plant the royal forests, and Carlos III built two country houses for his elder sons in clearings among the trees, both buildings surrounded by exquisite gardens.

A few kilometres north of El Escorial rises the silhouette of the granite Santa Cruz del Valle de los Caídos (the Holy Cross of the Valley of the Fallen), erected as a memorial to those who died in the Spanish Civil War. Since Republican prisoners of war had worked on the monument, it is dedicated to those who fell fighting on both sides. A funicular railway takes you from the modern and ponderous Benedictine monastery (whose chapel, 262 metres long, takes the form of a tunnel excavated out of the rock) to the foot of the cross, which stands 150 metres high. Here General Franco, who died clutching an arm of St Teresa of Avila, which had accompanied him everywhere since 1937, chose to be buried. Franco also arranged for the body of the young founder of the Falange, José Antonio Primo de Rivera, to be buried in the Valle de los Caídos.

The N600 continues to climb the Sierra de Guadarrama towards Segovia, in winter through sometimes hazardous snowstorms. This is superb skiing country, and the resort of Navacerrada has an international slope 3520 metres long which descends 754 metres. The N601 winds tortuously over the mountain range, rising to 1860 metres above sea level; the driver breathes more easily after the peak, when the descent through the trees is often accompanied by rain rather than by snow.

Eleven kilometres before Segovia is La Granja de San Ildefonso. Its name derives from a farm or grange run by monks at the centre of royal hunting grounds. Here in 1721 Felipe V, the first Bourbon king of Spain,

The approach to the massive underground church in the Valle de Los Caidos.

Left **Monumental water gardens and statuary at La Granja de San Ildefonso.**

Above **A dog enjoys a siesta in the Plaza Mayor of Pedraza de la Sierra.**

179

commissioned Teodoro Ardemáns to build him a palace in the French style. In fact its façade agreeably mingles French classicism with Spanish Baroque. Felipe lies with his queen in the baroque chapel, built by Alemán and Sabatini, which has an altar of marble, bronze and lapis lazuli.

Redecorated in the nineteenth century, the lush salons of the palace culminate in the throne room, with its view of the splendid classical French-style gardens, the upper gardens the haunt of deer and pheasants, the lower ones with their 26 enormous fountains and Great Cascade set against a backdrop of the sierra. Here too is a museum of tapestries collected by the monarchs since the time of Charles V. In this palace the reactionary statesman Don Francisco Tadeo, Duke of Calomarde, carrying a document signed by Ferdinando VII which would have prevented Isabella II from succeeding to the throne of Spain, was faced with a furious Infanta Carlota. She struck him in the face, at which Calomarde murmured, 'White hands cannot offend.' Nevertheless he tore up the document, and Isabel became queen of Spain in 1830.

Two villages to the north-east of Segovia are entrancing enough to merit a special visit. Pedraza de la Sierra is still surrounded by walls and dominated by a fifteenth-century fortress set on a peak. After Charles V had put the French king François I to rout at the battle of Pavia in 1525, he imprisoned the king and his sons in this castle. The Plaza Mayor of Pedraza de la Sierra is surrounded on three sides by houses whose balconies and upper storeys are supported on powerful pillars, some of whose capitals are sculpted with the coats of arms of hidalgos of the past. The fourth side is occupied by the parish church.

Slightly more remote, Sepúlveda lies 26 kilometres north of Pedraza de la Sierra, beside a deep meander of the Río Duratón. It is reached by way of the Castillo de Castilnovo, built in the *mudéjar* style in the twelfth century. As you approach Sepúlveda you spot first the tower of El Salvador, undoubtedly the finest of several romanesque churches in a village which in the Middle Ages possessed no fewer than fifteen. Built in 1093, El Salvador was embellished in the twelfth century with

an arcaded gallery. Steep streets, sometimes transforming themselves into steps, climb the hillside to the ruined castle, which was built on the site of a Roman camp. Another sign of the antiquity of the village is the twelfth-century towers which guard the renaissance Ayuntamiento in the charming Plaza Mayor.

At both Pedraza de la Sierra and Sepúlveda the local speciality is *cordero asado* (roast lamb), often cooked over wood. In the cold season the soup of these parts is particularly welcome, and compares in quality with the full-bodied *sopa de pescado* of Salamanca. This is the authentic *sopa de ajo castellana*, reeking of garlic and laced with pepper, in which an egg poaches itself under slices of dunked bread.

The *alcázar* and the cathedral dominate Segovia itself, which stands on a rocky spur between the rivers Eresma and Clomores, whose confluence is immediately below the castle. Here in 1188 Alfonso VI of Castile set about extending a fortress begun by Abd ar-Rahman III, Caliph of Córdoba, and he also rebuilt the Roman walls around what was then scarcely more than a village. His walls and three of their ancient gateways remain, but the *alcázar* was almost entirely rebuilt in the mid fourteenth century by Enrique II of Castile, and in its present form dates mainly from a reconstruction after a fire in 1862. What did survive from the fourteenth century were the enormous moat and two mighty towers: the Torre de Juan Segundo and the even more impressive Torre del Homenaje, with its round defensive turrets.

The *alcázar* was occupied in 1474 by Enrique IV, on the decisive occasion when he led his sister Isabella through the streets of Segovia to proclaim her future queen of Castile. As yet, however, its famous spiky silhouette was still to be built; it was the work of Felipe II, who in the sixteenth century ordered the whole building to be roofed in slate. Now a museum, it is worth visiting in my view not so much for its tapestries and old furniture as simply for its architecture, particularly the Mozarabic ceiling of the Sala del Solio,

The dramatic gorge of the Río Duratón near Sepúlveda.

Segovia: welcome shade in Calle de Velarde, near the alcázar.

or throne room. From the plaza in front of the massive fortress you can look across the valley of the Eresma to the formidable landscape beyond, with the monastery of El Parral, the church of La Vera Cruz, the convent of Carmelitas Descalzas and the sanctuary of Nuestra Señora de la Fuencisla spread out below.

Segovia is a warren of twisting streets, romanesque churches and a magnificent gothic cathedral. From the *alcázar*, take the picturesque Calle de Daioz to the Plaza de la Merced and the church of San Andrés, with its twelfth-century romanesque apse and its brick romanesque belfry, the rest restored and austere. As you approach it along the curving street you pass a couple of romanesque doorways and then a gothic one. The ancient gateway in the city walls to the south-east of this church is named after the church, the Puerta de San Andrés. (The other two twelfth-century gates still standing are the Puerta de Santiago and the Puerta de San Cebrián.) A plaque here celebrates the characters created by Castile's seventeenth-century poet and novelist Francisco Gómez de Quevedo y Villegas, whose finest work is the picaresque tale *Buscón Pablos*. Quevedo was bold enough to write verses urging Felipe IV to care for the common people, for which he was imprisoned in a monastery at León.

From San Andrés, Calle Marqués del Arco climbs to Segovia's cathedral, the last great gothic church in Spain. It stands at the highest point of the city, and was built to replace a cathedral almost completely demolished by the *comuneros* in 1520. Juan Gil de Hontañón and his son Rodrigo, who were also working on the cathedral at Salamanca, began the building in 1525, when Bishop Diego de Ribera laid the cornerstone. The following year Juan died and his son assumed total responsibility for the work. The foundation stone of the nave was laid in 1567.

The huge basilica, with its dome 67 metres high, is supported by flying buttresses with delicately sculpted pinnacles. Mini-transepts scarcely protrude beyond the aisles, and seven polygonal chapels of 1593 radiate from its apse. Walk round to the north side to discover the plateresque patio of the Casa del Marqués del Arco and to the south side to admire the cloisters, which shelter the canons from the midday sun. So, inside the cathedral, do the lovely late gothic stained glass windows.

Complex ogival ribs support the roof of the nave, and the webbed vaulting of the sanctuary, ornamented with sculpted bosses, is even more elaborate. As usual, the choir occupies the centre of the cathedral, forming a church within a church. Double rows of gothic stalls carved in mahogany – 118 in all, some of them dating from the fifteenth century – flank this choir. The baroque lectern, which dates from the seventeenth century, rests on a mahogany base carved in the plateresque style. The choir faces the Capilla Mayor, whose reredos dates from the 1770s, though it incorporates a thirteenth-century statue of Our Lady of

The cathedral and *alcázar* of Segovia, seen from the west.

Peace. In spite of its name, King Ferdinando II used to take it along whenever he set off to wage war.

In the north aisle is a doorway dedicated to St Frutos, one of the city's patron saints. His relics lie in a bronze urn in the central niche of the trascoro. Some of the chapels on either side of this portal should not be missed on even the most cursory visit. In the first to the west, the Capilla de la Piedád, Juan de Juni's dramatic interpretation of the Deposition, carved in 1571, has given each participant a distorted and exaggerated expression, the most animated reserved for the Roman soldier who seems about to cry, 'Truly this was the son of God.' Even God the Father, in a medallion, is shown to be suffering, wiping his brow with his right arm. Beside this reredos is a Flemish triptych of the Deposition, painted in the 1530s by Ambrosio Benson, who came from Lombardy but had learned his skills in Flanders.

An altar-piece dedicated to the patrons of Segovia gives pride of place to the Virgin of Fuencisla, an image said to have been responsible for saving the life of a young Jewish girl, falsely accused of infidelity with a Christian and flung over a cliff for her crime. St Frutos, his sister and his brother also appear in this altar-piece. A painting to the left depicts one of St Frutos's most entertaining miracles. Apparently the Moors, having occupied Segovia, were pursuing the poor citizens into the nearby desert where Frutos lived a solitary life (apart from the occasional company of his brother and sister). Frutos simply traced on the ground a line which transformed itself into an impassable chasm. On the right is depicted another quaint miracle. A mule, rather than eat a sack of barley in the presence of the exposed Host, kneels humbly before it, to the confusion of all unbelievers.

A fifteenth-century gothic grille made by Fr Francisco de Salamanca closes the Capilla de la Piedád, while the next chapel to the west, dedicated to St Andrew, is shielded by a screen wrought in the

Delicate ribs above the south aisle of the cathedral, Segovia.

God the Father blesses the world from this plateresque doorway in the cloister of Segovia cathedral.

seventeenth century. St Andrew, nailed to his X-shaped cross, appears in the classical reredos, which was made by Pedro de Brizuela in 1621. Next is a chapel with a reredos made by Gregorio Fernández in 1632, representing saints Cosmas and Damien, the patron saints of doctors. And at the far end of this aisle is the Capilla de la Concepción, the oddest in the whole cathedral. Here a skeleton wields a hammer, and golden words issue from the mouth of a man: TIBI SOLI PECCAVI ('Against you only I have sinned'). Still more alarming is a painting on the opposite wall of the Tree of Life. In the branches seventeenth-century revellers are dancing and feasting, oblivious of the fact that the devil in the form of a skeleton has almost chopped through the whole trunk with his scythe, while one of his demon assistants has a rope ready to pull them all into everlasting flames. Fortunately Jesus is anxiously ringing a bell with a hammer to warn the revellers that their time is nearly up.

Walk back towards the ambulatory, passing the Puerta de San Frutos, to the chapel of St Anthony Abbot, whose huge baroque reredos shows the saint as a bearded figure carrying a shepherd's crook and, as is traditional in depictions of him, accompanied by a pig. At the other side of the ambulatory is a chapel which in architectural extravagance exceeds all that we have yet seen. The Capilla del Sagrario, with its cruel statue of Jesus in Agony, leads into the Capilla Ayala, which was designed by José de Churriguera in the late seventeenth century. It has a cupola open to the skies, and its exuberant reredos fills the whole of the east end.

One other chapel should not be missed before you enter the cathedral cloisters. Passing a doorway topped by a fourteenth-century crucifixion scene (which came from the former cathedral), you find the Capilla de Santiago in the middle of the south aisle. Its renaissance reredos depicts the miraculous intervention in the battle of Clavijo of St James the Great, enabling the Christians to defeat the Moors. This is a more detailed reredos than many devoted to St James, for it also depicts him swimming to the shore at his risen Lord's command – even though the gospel of John tells us it was Simon Peter who did this. Jesus on the shore is cooking fish on a fire, to show that he is no ghost and needs breakfast like everyone else. The reredos also illustrates the beheading of St James, and shows bullocks pulling a cart containing his dead body. This little scene is of great importance in the legend of St James, for the bullocks are carrying his exhumed corpse to be reinterred not in Jerusalem but in Galicia. Above these scenes he is depicted alive again, dressed as a pilgrim to Santiago de Compostela. Francisco de Gutiérrez de Cuéllar, who commissioned this reredos in the early seventeenth century, appears in a portrait bust, dressed as a knight of Santiago.

The cathedral cloisters are entered through a gothic doorway in the Capilla del Cristo del Consuelo, which stands just to the east of the Capilla de Santiago. On one of the tombs in this chapel lies the effigy of Bishop Diego de Covarrubias, whom we have already seen at Toledo, painted by El Greco at the burial of Count Orgaz. The superb portal here, together with its Pietà, was carved in the fifteenth century by Juan de Guas and survived the sack of the former cathedral.

The cloisters too represent a remarkable survival. Using mostly materials cannibalized from the former cathedral, Juan de Campero created this exquisite gothic paradise in the early sixteenth century, following the lines of the original cloisters built by Juan de Guas in the 1460s.

Here is the last resting place of María del Salto, the Jewess accused of adultery and saved by the Virgin of Fuencisla. She finally died a natural death in 1237. The cloisters also house a thirteenth-century byzantine Crucifix and the tombs of the two cathedral architects. Over the grave of Rodrigo Gil de Hontañón (which is scarcely noticeable among the elegant tombs of canons) a simple slab records the date when the first stone of the cathedral was laid. Off the cloister is the chapter-house, which has a sixteenth-century gilded and white-painted coffered ceiling, and is hung with Flemish tapestries based on cartoons by Rubens. They depict the history of Queen Zenobia of Palmyra. This remarkable woman had married a Bedouin who in AD 264 was recognized by the Emperor Gallienus as governor of the city. When her husband was assassinated, Zenobia assumed power and soon conquered almost all of Rome's eastern provinces. Her court was filled with soldiers and intellectuals, the star among the latter her secretary Longinus, said by his contemporaries to be 'a living library and a walking museum'. Possibly a convert to Judaism, she also supported a maverick Christian bishop of Antioch, Paul of Samosta, who kept a choir of ladies to serenade him as if he were an angel. Eventually her armies were conquered by the Emperor Aurelian and Zenobia was brought to Antioch in chains. The tapestry depicting her submission to the emperor also portrays her dog snarling at him. Astutely she blamed her secretary for the war, and he was beheaded. Zenobia's chains were replaced by jewels,

The spiky east end of Segovia cathedral.

and after a triumphal entry into Rome she lived in affluent retirement at Tivoli.

A staircase decked with Flemish tapestries leads up from the cloister to the Diocesan Museum, whose delights include paintings by José de Ribera and the pupils of Pedro Berruguete. A silver-gilt altar-piece designed by Benvenuto Cellini has Jesus positively leaping from his tomb. A huge silver monstrance stands on a seventeenth-century baroque carriage pulled by a sculpted bull and a sculpted lion. Both the monstrance and the gilded carriage are the work of Rafael González. Paraded through the streets during the feast of Corpus Christi, the bells on the monstrance ring as it rocks. Also in the museum is the tomb of the Infante Don Pedro, the two-year-old son of Enrique II who died in 1366 when his nurse dropped him by mistake from a window of the *alcázar*. Sculpted on his tomb, the little lad lies holding on to his sword.

At Segovia the *alcázar*, as well as the Virgin Mary, once sheltered Jews alongside Christians and Moors. A street named Judería Vieja, leading from the east end of the cathedral, indicates the quarter where they lived, a ghetto near the city walls and stretching from Piazza Socorro to the Palacio de los Condes de Alpuente. As at Toledo, where the medieval synagogue was transformed into the church of Santa María la Blanca, so in Segovia the architectural legacy of the Sephardic Jews of Spain has been to some extent effaced in the *mudéjar* church of Corpus Cristi, once Segovia's synagogue. It was partly rebuilt, with three naves, after a fire of 1899, and the restoration was carried out with a regrettable clumsiness that destroyed some superb capitals, but the arches and the larchwood roof remain authentically Moorish.

Judería Vieja joins Calle Isabel la Católica, part of the pedestrianized quarter of Segovia and one of its most entrancing streets. Turn right and walk along to Calle Juan Bravo, which is named after a leader of the *comuneros* who was killed in 1571. Today this pedes-trianized thoroughfare, which climbs almost from Segovia's aqueduct to the Plaza Mayor, is much favoured for evening walks, and around nine o'clock it is filled with parading families, couples holding hands and groups of giggling schoolchildren. Then they repair to the restaurants to sample beans and pigs' ears, or Cantimpalo sausage, finishing likely as not with a *ponche segoviano*, a cake soaked with orange liqueur and topped with marzipan.

From Calle Juan Bravo a wide flight of steps climbs up to the twelfth-century romanesque church of San Martín, one of the finest in Segovia. An impressive building, with a three-storey belfry topped with a pointed steeple, it has porticoes on three sides, the capitals on the south side entwined with sculpted flowers and fanciful beasts. The beautiful golden stone has not weathered well, and the best-preserved capitals are those sheltered by the romanesque portico while the most intricate carvings are those over the main doorway. Those around the west door are equally seductive, if alas crumbling, and those on the columns of the north side are magnificent. Scenes from the Old and New Testaments are matched by episodes in later church history and mythology. The Old Testament figures include King David, traditionally the author of the psalms and therefore surrounded by musicians. From the life of Jesus the sculptors have depicted the Annunciation, Mary and Joseph on their way to Bethlehem, the resurrection of Lazarus, the Last Supper, Palm Sunday and the entry of Jesus into Jerusalem, Judas betraying his Lord with a kiss and finally a Christ in Majesty. Later episodes in Christian history are represented by a Mass of St Martin of Tours and by the mythical combat between the giant Ferragut and Charlemagne's peer Roland, while the medieval imagination reveals itself in a scene in which two knights battle with a monster.

In a plateresque chapel of 1549 in the south aisle hangs a fifteenth-century painting of the Virgin Mary appearing to St Ildefonso. Birds, beasts, men and angels scramble among the leaves of the doorway to this chapel, which was built by Juan de Guas. His chapel also encloses two alabaster tombs by the Herrera

---

Barley-sugar columns rise in a patio in Segovia off Calle Juan Bravo.

family. A statue in the chapel to the right of the Capilla Mayor is the work of Gregorio Fernández and depicts Jesus hideous in death. In this church too is a medieval statue of the Virgin Mary with long flowing hair, standing on a crescent moon; it was carved by Felipe Aragón in 1629. A sculpted figure of the Mater Dolorosa stands in a plateresque niche in the right-hand wall and, on the reredos of the main altar, St Martin of Tours slices his cloak in two.

Plazuela San Martín extends around the apse of the church, surrounded by ancient houses with loggias on their upper storeys and guarded by the machicolated Lozoya tower. Look out for what are probably romanesque sculptures of bulls (though in their present worn state they could easily be hippos). A bronze statue of Juan Bravo dates from 1921, his hand resolutely grasping the hilt of his sword.

From the front of the church, Calle de Infanta Isabel runs to Segovia's Plaza Mayor, a plaque on the wall of the *calle* identifying the spot where on 13 December 1474 Isabella was proclaimed queen of Castile. The plaza itself, the hub of a number of curving streets, is arcaded and usually dotted with market stalls. On one side is the classical Teatro Juan Bravo of 1917. This is the focal point of the city's festivities: at carnival time men in sombreros and ponchos play guitars as they process around the square, leading young people performing a redskin war dance, and processions of both young and old in silver and gold masks and all manner of flamboyant costumes. Between 24 and 29 June the Plaza Mayor again bursts into life for the festivals of San Juan and San Pedro, an occasion that also calls for bullfights.

Here too stand the Herreran town hall, built between 1610 and 1630, and the church of San Miguel, famed for its baroque retables. Rodrigo Gil de Hontañón built the church in 1558, though the thirteenth-century doorway and old pillars derive from a former church which stood on this site.

Inside, white plastered walls show off the sandstone pillars, from which springs ogival vaulting. Though it carries a sculpture of St Michael slaying the dragon, the classical reredos of the high altar pales beside the baroque ones in the chapels to its left and right. On one of them blood runs down the corpse of Jesus, who is supported by his mother, St John the Evangelist and a beseeching Mary Magdalene, while cherubs carry the instruments of his passion. The other depicts Our Lady and illustrates scenes from the Old and New Testaments in seventeenth-century baroque style. But these reredoses are not the only treasures of San Miguel. In the first chapel to the right is a chiaroscuro entombment scene. On the same side, the Capilla del Santísimo has an alabaster tomb with gothic inscriptions and the effigies of a knight and his lady. One flank of the sepulchre is carved with Jesus's crucifixion and the other with his entombment.

From the north-west corner of the Plaza Mayor, wend your way up to another splendid romanesque church, colonnaded on two sides and dedicated to San Esteban. Its bell tower itself is a romanesque masterpiece; the two lower storeys have blank arches and are topped by three more storeys whose open arches grow more graceful as the belfry rises. The Segovians dub it 'the queen of Spanish towers'. Inside is a plateresque side chapel, and cockle shells decorate the vaulting. Christ appears in a mandorla on the middle capital of the east end.

Segovia's episcopal palace, built in the sixteenth and seventeenth centuries, stands beside the church of San Esteban, and from here a rewarding walk along Calle de la Trinidád reveals first the plateresque façade of the Casa de Diego Victoria and then the convent of Santo Domingo. The latter has a massive corbelled tower known as the Torre de Hércules, since its romanesque sculptures include one of Hercules threatening a wild boar. Storks have made their rickety nest on its roof. Across the road is the romanesque church of La Trinidád, with a square belfry and an upper storey of attractive pink stone.

Make your way back to Calle Juan Bravo and at the end you will see a remarkable fortified house. The

A typical romanesque loggia, part of the church of San Esteban at Segovia.

fourteenth-century Casa de los Picos derives its name from the beak-shaped stones (or *picos*) with which its façade was clad in the sixteenth century, a decorative device which was also designed to deflect missiles.

Then, following Calle Cervantes, the visitor is suddenly plunged into Roman Segovia. Scarcely any Roman remains in Spain match in size the aqueduct (*El Puente*, as the Segovians call it) which rises above the lively Plaza del Azoguejo. Built under Augustus Caesar, this massive arcaded structure of huge blocks of granite – fitted together without benefit of mortar – was restored at the time of the Emperor Trajan who ruled from AD 98 to 117. In spite of the colossal stones from which it was made, the aqueduct is one of the most graceful constructions in the city. It rises on two tiers to a height of 26·5 metres and consists of a total of 167 arches stretching for 728 metres.

The Moors demolished 35 of its arches when they besieged the city in 1071. Isabella of Castile commissioned Juan Escovedo to restore them, and he did so following the pattern of the old Roman architects. Until the early twentieth century the city depended on the water brought by the aqueduct from the Río Frío, 17 kilometres away. Skilfully the Romans achieved an almost uniform slope of 1 in 100, down which the waters flowed to Segovia.

Naturally the Christians were unwilling to concede that the pagan Romans could have created such a wonder, and a legend grew up that a girl, whose job it was to carry water across the valley to the city, sold her soul to the devil provided that he brought the stream over to Segovia in one night. The devil agreed and began building the aqueduct. At the last moment the girl repented and begged the Blessed Virgin to save her. Mary obliged by causing the cocks to crow just before Satan had finished his work. The Segovians thus inherited a virtually complete aqueduct and the water-carrier saved her soul.

Just as the Zocodover at Toledo derives from the

Symbol of ancient Rome, this modern statue of the she-wolf suckling Romulus and Remus stands beside the aqueduct built at Segovia under Augustus Caesar.

Arabic *sucq*, meaning market, so does the name of the Plaza del Azoguejo. Avenida Fernández Ladreda runs south-east from this square, passing the romanesque church of San Clemente on its way to San Millán. Pause at San Clemente, whose chief treasures are the thirteenth-century frescoes which decorate the walls and vault of the chapel on the right of the Capilla Mayor, among their subjects Christ in Majesty and a Tree of Jesse which culminates in the Madonna. A colonnade flanks one side of the church, and its tower is square and defensive.

The romanesque church of San Millán has a superb *mudéjar* tower, built between 1110 and 1123, semicircular apses and colonnaded porticoes to north and south. The carvings are in fairly good condition, though I find it hard to make out the subject of the group over the doorway. The font dates from the ninth century; while the splendid baroque barrel vault can

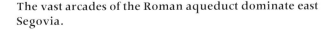

The vast arcades of the Roman aqueduct dominate east Segovia.

be faulted only because it conceals a Mozarabic ceiling. An idea of what is hidden here can be gained by walking further south-east, to the monastery of San Antonio el Real, which occupies a palace founded in 1455 by Enrique IV of Castile. Its gothic chapel has a magnificent *mudéjar* ceiling painted in red, blue and gold.

How many romanesque churches does one city need? North of the aqueduct, the twelfth-century San Justo has frescoes nearly as fine as those in San Clemente, as well as a contemporary statue of Jesus brought here from Gascony and used in Holy Week processions. And running north-west from the Plaza del Azoguejo, Calle San Juan takes us to the romanesque church of San Juan de los Caballeros. A triple apse, a colonnade and splendid decoration make it well worth a visit. The church has become an art gallery dedicated to the works of the twentieth-century painter Ignacio Zuloaga, friend of Gauguin and Degas, and the ceramics of his brother Daniel.

Paseo de la Cruz runs past the former convent of Santa Cruz; this time the church is gothic, restored in the 1820s after a fire. Ferdinand and Isabella founded the convent, and following their custom had themselves sculpted on the west portal, along with the crucified Jesus, while their motto, *Tanto monta*, is carved inside and outside the building. Oddly enough, no-one is sure what this motto signifies. Does it mean 'onward and upward', or is it meant to explain that Ferdinand of Aragón was equal to Isabella of Castile? The Catholic Kings also had their crowned initials and their symbols of arrows and a yoke carved on the church. Storks cheekily nest on this royal foundation.

Another romanesque church, San Lorenzo, rises a little way to the east. San Lorenzo has a triple apse and a delightful tower with decorated brickwork. Like San Martín and San Juan de los Caballeros, it is enhanced by colonnades, these ones very graceful, with rich capitals. Romanesque faces peer down from under the tiles above the arcades.

Dating from early twelfth century, San Millán is one of the oldest romanesque churches in Segovia.

To find the imposing monastery of El Parral (which means arbor of vines) you have to cross the River Alameda. Juan Gallego began building its church and Juan de Guas took over in 1472; the tower was finished some fifty years later. Calle del Marques de Vielena runs south from here, still on the far side of the river, with the *alcázar* towering up to the left, and then turns back on itself to the romanesque church of La Vera Cruz. Built on the site of a Roman temple, it was founded in 1208 by the Knights Templars and it follows their favourite pattern, the twelve-sided church of the Holy Sepulchre in Jerusalem. Beside this dodecagon is a square tower, and the church boasts what I believe to be the only doorway in Segovia with dog-tooth decoration. Inside is a little central chapel surrounded by a vaulted ambulatory.

At the other side of the street rise the walls of the convent of the Carmelitas Descalzas, founded in 1586 by one of Spain's greatest mystics, St John of the Cross. He lies buried today inside the convent chapel, which opens off a simple renaissance cloister. St John was not only co-founder with St Teresa of the Discalced Carmelites (so-called because they wore sandals rather than shoes); he was also a Castilian poet whose lyrical religious mysticism exceeded even the spiritual intensity of the works of Lope de Vega. Born at Fontiveros (about 60 km east of Salamanca) in 1542 into an extremely poor family, he found work in a hospital at the age of 17 so as to be able to pursue his education with the Jesuits of Medina del Campo. In 1563 he became a novice Carmelite monk, continuing his education for the next five years at the university of Salamanca. Ordained towards the end of this period, he then met St Teresa who confided to him her desire to restore a new discipline to the Carmelites. The two joined forces, the young priest changed his name to John of the Cross, and both now began lives of austerity and contemplation.

Their reform provoked so much hostility that early in December 1577 unreformed Carmelites kidnapped the saint, and when he refused to recant his commitment to his new regime they imprisoned him at Toledo, where for nine months he lived in a dark cell scarcely 2

metres wide and 3 metres long. Paradoxically, it was here that he composed some of his finest poems, before escaping in August 1578.

Four works sum up his teaching and express both his ecstasy and his torment. These are *The Ascent of Mount Carmel, Dark Night of the Soul*, a mystical discourse between the soul and Jesus which he called *The Spiritual Canticle*, and *The Living Flame of Love*.

In his teachings he explains that in order to ascend to the spiritual heights of Mount Carmel and receive there a vision of God, every appetite must be mortified, for a Christian's senses, he believed, are a gift to be used only for the honour and glory of God and as a means of imitating Jesus. He teaches his readers how to contemplate, even when the soul is walking apparently blindly, in darkness illuminated only by faith. So *The Ascent* leads naturally on to the two books which describe the dark night of the soul. As you read *The Spiritual Canticle* it becomes clear that the saint is writing entirely from personal experience; he describes his anxious search for his beloved Saviour and his first meetings with him, which eventually lead to perfect union – a union that will become even more glorious after death. The verses of *The Living Flame of Love* meditate passionately on the highest form of union with God that anyone can attain while still on earth. And yet they reveal that this desire for union

Ferdinand and Isabella are sculpted along with the crucified Jesus on the façade of the former convent of Santa Cruz.

with the divine is nothing self-indulgent, for it must be expressed not only in the virtues of faith and hope but also in that of charity.

St John of the Cross approached the fulfilment of his deep desire for death in September 1591, when a fever caused his leg to inflame into an ulcer. He nonetheless felt obliged to seek medical help, and left his solitary existence in southern Spain to go to Ubeda in Andalusia, where no-one knew him and no-one would disturb his mortifications and prayer. In the Carmelite priory of Ubeda, whose prior continually complained of the expense of keeping him there, St John of the Cross died on 13 December, repeating the psalm which his Saviour had used on the cross, 'Into thy hands I commend my spirit'.

The chapel in which he lies has been disfigured by a dreadful abstract reredos behind the high altar, painted by Gerardo Lopéz Bonilla in 1982. It allegedly represents elements in the teaching of John of the Cross. The body of the saint (or in truth only his head and trunk, for other bits of him bless altars elsewhere in Christendom) was transferred here from Ubeda two years after his death.

Across the wide square, whose stone benches are sheltered by trees, stands the far more imposing sanctuary of Nuestra Señora de la Fuencisla, built in thanksgiving to the mother of Jesus after she had saved Maria del Salto from certain death. Behind the church rises the cliff over which the Jewess was thrown. The Segovians call it the *Peña Grajera*, the cliff of the crows, which still fly in and out of the holes in the rock face, cawing loudly.

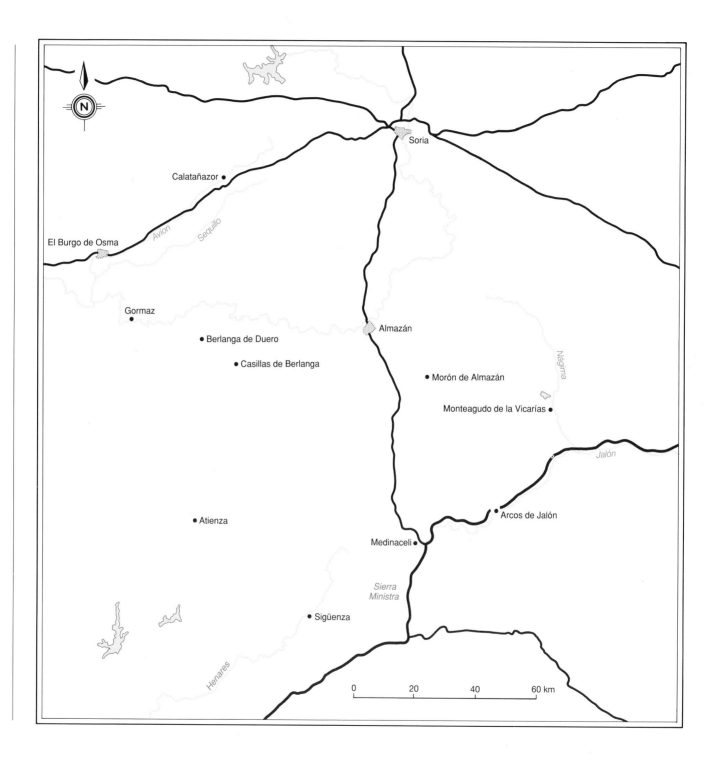

Calatañazor ●

El Burgo de Osma ●

Soria

Gormaz ●

● Berlanga de Duero

● Casillas de Berlanga

Almazán

● Morón de Almazán

Monteagudo de la Vicarías ●

Arcos de Jalón ●

● Atienza

Medinaceli ●

Sierra
Ministra

● Sigüenza

Avion

Sequillo

Nágima

Jalón

Henares

0   20   40   60 km

7
The Eastern Reaches of the Duero

Sigüenza – Medinaceli – El Burgo de Osma – Soria

The Spanish are in the habit of declaring certain exceptional towns and villages national monuments, and none deserves that honour more than Sigüenza, in the province of Guadalajara. Its *alcázar*, now a National Parador, looks down from a hill on to the left bank of the poplar-lined Río Henares; and tumbling down the hillside, palaces, convents, churches and ancient houses overlook the Henares valley. The city is served by an eighteenth-century aqueduct which reaches almost to the Plaza Mayor, with its porticoed houses and renaissance Ayuntamiento.

Of all the fine buildings of Sigüenza the gem is the cathedral, also in the Plaza Mayor. Bishop Bernardo d'Agen, a Frenchman, began building it in the mid twelfth century, when the city had been taken from the Moors, though the cathedral was not finished until the fifteenth century. The masons too were French, apparently from the region of Poitiers. To defend its sober façade, on which is sculpted a medallion depicting the Virgin Mary offering St Ildefonso his celebrated chasuble, they built two thickset defensive towers modelled on those of Poitiers cathedral, each with a stair turret. For the south transept they created in the next century a magnificent rose window.

You find your way inside through a doorway in the Plaza del Obispo Don Bernardo, which is flanked by a sixteenth-century tower. Twenty-four piers, each one with a cluster of twenty shafts whose capitals are carved with romanesque foliage, support the arcades. Sigüenza cathedral also boasts two pulpits, which are quite different in style though both are alabaster, the one on the left carved in 1495, the one on the right dating from 1572. A low lantern, put up after the destruction of the crossing vault in the Civil War, filters the light into the south transept.

A grille made around 1630 shields the Capilla Mayor and its tombs, which include a splendid one of Cardinal Carillo de Albornoz (who died in 1434) as well as those of his parents and a number of bishops. Giraldo de Merío was responsible for its early seventeenth-century reredos. The flamboyant gothic stalls in the choir are in part by Rodrigo Alemán. Behind the choir, a sumptuously baroque marble tras-coro enshrines a twelfth-century statue of the Virgin Mary, which was covered in silver 300 years later.

Undoubtedly the finest monument in the cathedral is the gothic tomb of Don Martín Vázquez de Arce, in the chapel of San Juan in the south transept. Military commander of the city in the second half of the fifteenth century, he was only 25 when he perished fighting the Moors outside Granada in 1486. Perhaps because of his boyish face, he is quaintly known as the Doncel, a term normally used only for young pages at a fifteenth-century court. Dressed in chain mail and

199

with a splendid cloak around his shoulders, Don Martín lies half recumbent on his alabaster tomb, supporting himself on one elbow as he reads a book, while a pageboy sits at his feet. He seems likely to look up at any moment and gaze across from his niche at the figures lying on sepulchres just beyond his own. They include other members of the Arce family, the finest statue being that of Bishop Fernando de Arce, who died in 1521.

No-one should neglect several other chapels in the cathedral, above all the renaissance Capilla de Santa Librada (patron saint of the town) which Alonso de Covarrubias built in the north transept. Don Fadrigue of Portugal lies here in an early sixteenth-century tomb. Among the other chapels worth visiting are the Capilla de San Pedro, with a plateresque grille by Juan Francés, the Capilla de la Anunciación, with a *mudéjar* entrance, and the Capilla de San Marcos, whose fifteenth-century triptych is by Francisco de Rincón. Even now the jewels of this cathedral are not yet exhausted. Covarrubias built a splendid sacristy, which is accessible from the ambulatory, its coffered ceiling decorated with a rose design and incorporating 300 medallions. The late gothic cloisters were begun in 1507 under the patronage of Cardinal Bernardo Carvajál and finished in 1623.

Before exploring the rest of the city, spare time for the Museo Diocesano de Arte Antiguo, which displays romanesque sculptures, plateresque reredoses, a brilliant Assumption by El Greco and an Immaculate Conception by Zurbarán. Of the churches of Sigüenza, Santiago has an excellent romanesque porch. Medieval Calle Mayor leads to the Travesaña Alta, through which is the Plaza de San Vicente, whose romanesque church has a baroque reredos. In this same square stands the fifteenth-century house of the Doncel.

So proud are the citizens of Sigüenza of their former Doncel that they have named their special brand of sugared egg-yolk after him, and *yemas del Doncel* are

Sigüenza cathedral rises at the end of Calle de los Martires.

These brass spouts of a horse trough lie in the shadow of Sigüenza cathedral.

on sale everywhere. Other gastronomic specialities here are breaded river crab and quail with pepper.

Sigüenza's Plaza Mayor has renaissance porticoes and, on one side, the renaissance Ayuntamiento. Those with a taste for more churches will relish the renaissance Nuestra Señora de los Huertos, with a praying statue by Master Juan, who created the Doncel's tomb in the cathedral. San Francisco is a baroque building, while the eighteenth-century seminary church of San Jerónimo contains some tombs of the dukes of Medinaceli, who took their name from the next-but-one stop on our tour.

The walled town of Atienza, north-west of Sigüenza, is celebrated for a crucial moment in 1162 when the citizens rallied to the cause of the child king Alfonso VIII and saved him from falling into the clutches of his uncle and rival, Ferdinando II of León. Annually, on the Sunday before Pentecost, the present inhabitants of Atienza dress in medieval costume and

commemorate that episode in Castilian folklore with a fiesta known as La Caballada (the cavalcade). Perched on a rocky plateau above the town, the ruined twelfth- and thirteenth-century fortress, with its two curtain walls and keep, was a major bastion of defence during the reconquest of Castile from the Moors. Atienza has no fewer than five medieval churches (though Santa María del Rey is in ruins). The romanesque church of San Gil, with a fine semicircular apse, has become a little local museum, while San Juan was transformed at the renaissance and later given a churrigueresque reredos. The secular architecture of Atienza is equally ravishing. Plaza del Trigo is surrounded by houses whose balconies rest on columns decorated with coats of arms, and the Plaza del Ayuntamiento, entered by way of the romanesque Arrebatacapas arch, is enclosed by fifteenth-century houses.

Across the stony Sierra Ministra to the north-east of Sigüenza, pink-stoned Medinaceli rises on a promontory overlooking the Río Jalón. The name of the dukes and that of the town derive from the Arabic *Medina Salim*, for this spot was once a Moorish stronghold. Even earlier it was a Roman camp, and the Romans have bequeathed to Medinaceli a third-century triumphal arch, the only one in Spain to have retained its three openings. No fewer than forty Medinaceli tombs are housed in the sixteenth-century collegiate church of Santa María, which has a baroque reredos. The family built itself an eighteenth-century palace bordering the arcaded Plaza Mayor, which still retains its old corn market, now the cultural and tourist headquarters.

Each November the citizens host a festival known as the Toro Júbilo. The last creature to rejoice is the bull itself, which is here tormented with fire before being finally slain. For reasons which are difficult to fathom, the cult of the bullfight underwent an unexpected

The partially enclosed lower cloister of the Real Monasterio de Santa María de los Huertos, evidence that the Cistercians who built it in the twelfth century felt the need to be able to defend themselves.

revival in Spain during the 1980s, and now some 3000 magnificent animals are slaughtered annually in this ritual fashion. In his *Death in the Afternoon* Ernest Hemingway pontificated that 'All of bullfighting is founded on the bravery of the bull, his simplicity, and his lack of experience', arguing that 'A cowardly bull is difficult to fight since he will not charge the picadors more than once if he receives any punishment and so is not slowed down.' During the Toro Júbilo of Medinaceli such words as cowardly can in no way be applied to the tortured beasts.

Seventeen kilometres north-east, through a gorge-slashed countryside of slate, limestone and gypsum, is the little town of Arcos de Jalón, remnants of whose medieval walls still stand. And after another 11 kilometres the royal monastery of Santa María de los Huertos rises beside the Río Jalón in the midst of a

Atienza, still guarded by its twelfth- and thirteenth-century fortress, was an important part of the defences of the Duero valley when the Christians were reconquering Spain from the Moors.

203

Palazuelos, a pretty walled village north of Sigüenza.

bizarre red terrain. Founded by Cistercians in 1162, this lovely fortified convent was inhabited by them continuously until 1835, when anticlericalists became dominant in Spain. Happily they returned in 1930. Over the centuries their buildings were enriched, so that today visitors enter by Herreran cloisters which were begun in 1582 and finished half a century later. The two statues in the cloister garden represent Archbishop Ximénez of Toledo and St Martín of Finojosa (abbot of Santa María de Huerta), who lie entombed in the monastery church.

The monks have taken care to signpost a route through their monastery which takes you from this first cloister, the Claustro de la Hospedería, to the thirteenth-century gothic Claustro de Caballeros and then to the massive thirteenth-century kitchen, which abuts on the gothic refectory, built in 1215. To the west is an even earlier building, the hall of the lay brothers, dating from the twelfth century and supported by a central row of columns.

East of the refectory the so-called royal staircase of 1600 rises to the plateresque upper gallery of the cloister, built in 1531; the original carved wooden ceiling, in which biblical scenes mingle with events of Spanish history, still embellishes its north wing and the rest has been reproduced in plaster. The chapter-house on the south side houses a display of ecclesiastical vestments, and beyond it is a raised choir whose walnut stalls were carved in 1557 and whose classical organ dates from the seventeenth century.

From the cloister a flight of steps leads down into the romanesque church. Its high altar has a reredos of 1766. Fourteenth-century frescoes decorate a chapel on the south side of the apse, while on the north side stands the eighteenth-century sacristy. Here too are buried the grandson of El Cid and the founder of the monastery, the warrior Archbishop Rodrigo Ximénez de Rada of Toledo. You leave the church through a late eighteenth-century wrought-iron grille.

Leaving Santa María de Huerta, the N11 runs northeast through gentle rolling country, soon reaching the Río Nágima, where you turn sharp left towards the village of Monteagudo de la Vicarías. On the way, the little fifteenth-century stronghold of Torre de Martín González appears to the left, looking down on the hermitage of Nuestra Señora de la Torre. The ruined walls of Monteagudo de las Vicarías date from the sixteenth century. Its fifteenth-century *castillo* has a renaissance patio, and the gothic parish church has a sixteenth-century reredos.

Rising to a height of 1082 metres above sea level as it crosses the pass, the C116 reaches Morón de Almazán after 21 kilometres. This is an even more charming village than Monteagudo de las Vicarías, and its ochre-coloured Plaza Mayor encompasses a late fifteenth-century pillory, an Ayuntamiento of the same epoch and a renaissance palace. The gothic parish church of Nuestra Señora de la Asunción has plateresque reliefs and a tower of 1540. In the late fourteenth century the

The Castilian landscape south-east of Berlanga de Duero, with sunflowers ripe for harvesting.

village was the centre of the feudal domain of the French baron Baltrán du Guesclin, who in 1369 had sided with Enrique II of Trastámara in his quarrel with his brother Pedro el Cruel.

Almazán, 14 kilometres north-east, on the left bank of the Duero, was also part of Du Guesclin's domain. Created as a stronghold by the Moors, it was taken from them in 1128 by Alfonso I. Several gateways and parts of its twelfth-century walls remain intact. Once again the Plaza Mayor is exquisite, flanked on one side by the long façade of the Palacio de Hurtado de Mendoza, a building whose apparent architectural harmony embraces gothic, renaissance and classical elements. Beside it rises the quaint, thirteenth-century church of San Miguel; its romanesque altar depicts the martyrdom of Archbishop Thomas Becket of Canterbury. Not far away stands the church of San Vicente, its main doorway romanesque, its apse Mozarabic. Nuestra Señora del Campanario dates from the twelfth century but was rebuilt in the eighteenth.

Continuing due west, the C116 runs along the Duero valley towards the unspoiled village of Berlanga de Duero, whose name derives from the Roman Augusta Valeriana. The town sits below a fifteenth-century fortress with an imposing thirteenth-century curtain wall. The marquises of Berlanga built themselves a plateresque palace here, and the dukes of Frías built another in the renaissance style. Berlanga de Duero has a collegiate church, built by Juan Rasines de Burgos, whose late gothic architecture is just giving way to the renaissance. Among its most striking features are its ogival vaulting and walnut choir stalls, which were carved around 1580. In the Capilla Mayor, with its painted and sculpted gothic reredos, is a fifteenth-century plateresque tomb. A gothic reredos sculpted in 1449 graces the Capilla de Santa Ana, while the tomb of Bishop Tomás de Berlanga, who died in 1551, is in the last chapel on the south side of the church, the Capilla de los Christos.

Before driving north-east to El Burgo de Osma, make a brief excursion in the opposite direction to visit the early eleventh-century hermitage of San Baudelio in the little village of Casillas de Berlanga. This Mozarabic church has retained some fragmentary tenth- and late twelfth-century romanesque frescoes on the horseshoe arches of the gallery (the rest alas transported not only to the Prado but also to the USA). Unusually the arches spring from a central column which carries a pulpit.

On the way to El Burgo de Osma, another little excursion, west to Gormaz, is also worthwhile. Gormaz boasts a massive fortress which the Moors built in 965 and the Christians enlarged in the thirteenth and fourteenth centuries. Its curtain wall, which stretches for some 380 metres, is protected by 24 towers and pierced by two powerful gateways.

From here the route north crosses the Río Sequillo and finally brings us to El Burgo de Osma. Gastronomically the city could not be more different from Sigüenza. Its speciality is pork, and it even celebrates this with a pig-slaughtering festival held at the end of February and the beginning of March.

Since Visigothic times El Burgo de Osma, which rises on the bank of the Río Ucero, has been the seat of a bishop, and in consequence what is little more than a delightful village of 4600 inhabitants boasts a cathedral. San Pedro de Osma, who was a monk from Cluny in France, built its romanesque predecessor in the twelfth century, but the present gothic building was created out of the generosity and piety of Don Juan Dominique a century later. The main entrance alone displays the great church's gradual process of enrichment, for what began as a thirteenth-century doorway with three rows of sculpted arches was restored in 1483 and is today sheltered by a coffered, early seventeenth-century renaissance porch. Behind a balustrade above this doorway is a gothic rose window. Very early fourteenth-century statues decorate the south portal. The tower, built by Domingo Ondátegui between 1739 and 1744, is pure Spanish Baroque and entirely dominates El Burgo de Osma.

Once inside the three-aisled church you notice the same French elements, adapted to Spanish ways, that

Near the cathedral of El Burgo de Osma.

influenced the cathedral of Sigüenza. Single lancets light the apse. The clerestory windows rise above a string-course over the springing of the vaults, and above them again rise the pointed arches which have supported the roof for 600 years. The cloisters, begun by Juan de la Piedra in 1510, open at their south-east corner into the vestry, whose arched bays, rising from four delicate columns, were built early in the second half of the thirteenth century.

A filigree screen by Nicolás Francés protects the Capilla Mayor, and two masters can be detected at work on its renaissance reredos: Juan de Juñi, who sculpted the left-hand side, and Juan Picardo, who depicted the falling asleep of the Virgin Mary on the right. The choir of 1570 has the usual carved walnut stalls, these dating from 1589, while the trascoro has a reredos dedicated to St Mary Magdalene and sculpted by Pierre Picard and Juan de Logroño.

To pay for the chapel which Juan de Villanueva created in the ambulatory for Bishop Juan de Palofax, the bishop charged a tax on every pot of wine sold on the diocesan estates. The left-hand aisle gives on to more fine chapels, particularly that of San Ildefonso, which has gothic paintings set in a baroque reredos. San Pedro de Osma lies in a tomb of 1258 which is housed in a mid sixteenth-century chapel reached by an elegant staircase. Angels hold the pillow on which the saint lays his head, and the sides of the sarcophagus are completely covered with lively, remarkably naturalistic scenes from Pedro's life. I particularly like the episode in which a rider seems to be flying in the air above his steed.

Baroque eighteenth-century houses add their allure to the Plaza Mayor, as do the former hospice of San Augustín and the episcopal palace. Before leaving El Burgo de Osma, look out for the university of Santa Catalina (on the main road), with its plateresque façade and renaissance, two-storey patio. Then take the N122, which runs north-east beside the Río Avión to Calatañazor, its ruined fortress overlooking the gorge.

Sunset falls on a shepherds' hut at Calatañazor.

In this detail from the church portal of Santo Domingo at Soria heavenly musicians play blithely while shepherds learn of the birth of Jesus and innocent children are slaughtered on the orders of King Herod.

Half-timbered houses add charm to the streets of this picturesque walled village. In its Plaza Mayor is a gothic pillory, and the once romanesque, now gothic, church of Santa María houses a sixteenth-century reredos. Close by this village the Moslem leader Al Mansour was killed in a battle against the Christians of León in 1002.

Although set among unhappy twentieth-century buildings, the medieval city of Soria is perfectly preserved. It lies 22 kilometres north-east of Calatañazor, 1056 metres above sea level on the right bank of the Duero. Russet-tiled roofs match the prevailing colour of the surrounding countryside. For once the cathedral is not the major building, giving place to the magnificent thirteenth-century church of Santo Domingo. Again the French element that is so often a feature of the history and architecture of this part of

Castile is evident here; the foundress of this church was Eleanor of England, the wife of Alfonso VIII.

The main doorway of Santo Domingo has in its tympanum a relief depicting angels worshipping the Holy Trinity, flanked by the Virgin Mary and one of the prophets – or perhaps St Dominic himself. Sculpted on the elaborately decorated archivolts are, working from the inside outwards, heavenly musicians, the 24 elders of the Apocalypse, a Massacre of the Innocents, scenes from the lives of Jesus and his mother, and the story of the Passion. Scenes from the Old Testament adorn the worn capitals of a two-tier row of blind arcades spanning the west front, and in the pediment above, where the russet stone fades into grey, is a romanesque rose window. Churrigueresque reredoses adorn the chapels of the interior, whose nave is romanesque and sanctuary gothic.

At the west end of the church is the narrow Calle de la Aduana Vieja, whose houses include the eighteenth-century Casa de los Castejones, with its baroque doorway, the sixteenth-century palace of the Viscount de Eza and the renaissance Casa de los Rios Salcedo. At the end of this *calle* you come upon the sixteenth-century Palacio de Alcántara, and next to it the Diputación which houses a Celtic-Iberian museum, the Museo Numantino. Turn left here to discover the romanesque church of San Juan de Rabanera, built in the form of a Latin cross, with a cupola over the crossing. Its west doorway was brought here from the church of San Nicolás, which had fallen into ruin, and therefore depicts not San Juan but scenes from the life of St Nicholas of Myra. In the tympanum Nicholas receives gifts from Constantine the Great, and on the capitals to the right he performs four miracles. The capitals on the left portray scenes from the life of Jesus. In the left transept of the church is a baroque reredos. A thirteenth-century fresco, much mutilated, adorns the right transept, as well as a mid sixteenth-century plateresque reredos by Francisco de Agreda. Do not

The sumptuous façade of the sixteenth-century Palacio Gómara.

forget to walk around the outside of the building to admire its single apse, a couple of whose windows contain no glass but are filled with simple roundels and romanesque decoration.

Calle de San Juan runs north from the church towards the superb Palacio Gómara. Built in the late sixteenth century for the counts of Gómara, the 100-metres-long façade of the palace shades from the renaissance to the classical style and is surmounted by a pinnacle tower. Two huge giants flank the coat of arms above the mighty doorway, which rises on Doric pilasters. To the west, across Plaza de Ayllón, stands the palace in which in 1581 St Teresa of Avila founded a Carmelite convent. Its façade was created by Marcos de la Piedra in 1568; and its seventeenth-century chapel has a churrigueresque reredos.

To the east, Calle de Obispo Augustín descends from the convent to the cathedral of San Pedro. In truth San Pedro has been a cathedral only since 1935. First built as a twelfth-century romanesque church, it was rebuilt by the Basque architect Juan Martínez Mutio in 1548. The main doorway is plateresque. Apart from some romanesque altars, the three galleries of the cloisters are all that remain of the original building, and these are delightful, the capitals of their twin columns sculpted with vegetation, saints and fabulous beasts. The chapels inside the cathedral are well worth exploring, particularly for a splendid Flemish triptych of 1559 in the Capilla de San Saturio, and Francisco del Río's classical reredos in the Capilla Mayor, alongside which is another one in the mid sixteenth-century plateresque style.

Walk on past the cathedral for a magnificent panorama of the Duero gorge, and cross the river to reach the ruins of the monastery of San Juan de Duero, which the Knights Hospitallers of St John of Acre built in the twelfth century. These ruins stand today in an archaeological park which incorporates a neolithic menhir, and the romanesque church is a museum displaying among its other treasures some thirteenth-century Jewish tombstones. Its roofless cloister has delicately interlaced ogival arches, and in parts of the galleries are *mudéjar* arches shaped like keyholes.

The thirteenth-century urge to found monasteries and hermitages was strong at Soria, and on the same bank of the Duero the Templars founded the monastery of San Polo, whose early thirteenth-century chapel still stands. Still further south is an octagonal shrine dedicated to the anchorite San Saturio. You reach it by way of a poplar-lined avenue beside the river. Although the building seems likely at any moment to slide down into the Duero, it is in fact set firmly on rock. The eighteenth-century Sorian artist Antonio Zapata frescoed the interior, which has a baroque altar.

Oddly enough, although San Saturio is the patron saint of the city, Soria's chief annual fiesta begins on the Thursday nearest to 24 June, the feast of San Juan and the Mother of God. For five days the citizens, divided into five groups, process in regional dress, host pilgrimages, run a fair and indulge in bullfights.

From Saturio's shrine it is worth making your way

A spectacular landscape at Puentetoba, west of Soria.

back across the river and climbing the pine-clad hill on which the remains of the medieval castle stand. Here, in a spectacular position overlooking the city and the river below, is a National Parador named after Antonio Machado, Soria's favourite poet. Though he was born in Seville, he lived here between 1907 and 1913, and his wife, Leonor, is buried in the sixteenth-century gothic church of Nuestra Señora del Espino, on the road up to the Parador (its Capilla Mayor has a plateresque reredos). Machado described romantically the stunning panorama of the landscape around Soria:

Grey hillsides, russet outcrops,
Deep groves of oak trees,
Wild screes and bare ridges,
Where the crossbow arc of the Duero
Runs around Soria.

On that hillside I often find myself thinking of those defenders of the city who long ago must anxiously have scanned the horizon for hostile invaders, whether Roman, Visigoth, Moorish or Christian.

Index